ENDORSEMENTS

The first time I heard Graham teach it seemed as if an intravenous feeding tube had been connected directly into my spirit from the Holy Spirit. As I read *Manifesting Your Spirit*, the second book in Graham's *The Way of the Warrior* series, I had the strange sensation that it was happening again. Only now, having been in community with Graham for nearly 10 years, I know why. There are those who write about the things they know they should believe, and those who write of things they actually believe. Then there are those who write of what they are authentically becoming, releasing a word that breathes life, courage and faith into the reader. Graham is such a writer, and *Manifesting Your Spirit* is such a word.

David Crone
Senior Team Leader
The Mission, Vacaville, California

My advice is simple: without delay, see to it that you absorb the impartation and heart-warmth that Graham is now offering in *The Way of the Warrior* series. In my years, I have not known of a manuscript that would serve so effectively as a passport, providing both the instructions and mindset, enabling us to emigrate from the place where most of us live: Whine Country! Whining consists of bellyaching, whimpering, complaining and other behavior designed to gain illegal attention.

Manifesting Your Spirit, takes us by the hand, shows us both the boundary and the negative fruit of Whine Country, places a passport in our hand and then establishes a new comfort level that allows us to emigrate from the place where we have been living, entering in the Kingdom dimension.

This author, whom I have known personally for many years, lives authentically all that he is seeking to impart. The first of this series, *Qualities of a Spiritual Warrior*, sets the basis of conflict into the realm of character. Seldom does any writer see this as fundamental. Soul and Spirit defines the real battle ground.

I am quietly hopeful that this series on *The Way of the Warrior* may be the first of a reformational season, showing us how to effectively prepare and release ordinary men and women into the dimension of increasingly complex spiritual warfare. Mature and difficult problems that now face us will require the type of warrior that Graham envisions.

For me, the section on human weakness and the manner in which it is applied in the life of the warrior is more than worth the price of the book! No one could have given us such insight, until and unless it was made to be his own in existential reality.

Bob Mumford
Lifechangers

Those who are used to build the vital walls of witness that have been broken down by opposition and neglect must, as Nehemiah of old, have a sword in one hand and a trowel in the other. With these, Nehemiah could war against the enemy or work to build the foundations of old as the situation demanded. The warrior must be a worker and a worshiper as well. Graham Cooke has presented us with strategic helps in the warfare facing us and splendid instructions to the warriors as well.

Jack Taylor
Dimensions Ministries
Melbourne, Florida

Once again, Graham Cooke has hit the mark in accurately hearing and expressing the heart of God for the body of Christ in the present hour. In this second book of his new series, *The Way of the Warrior*, he clearly articulates one of the significant paradigm shifts in the Church, the shift related to spiritual warfare. You will be encouraged, envisioned, and emboldened by this book to stand in the power and presence of God to see victory in your life and circumstances. As with everything Graham writes… a must-read!

Jane Hansen
Aglow International

Graham's new book brings the presence of God, and the power of the Holy Spirit alive with many fresh insights. Graham is one of my most favorite people. You can read something he has written and realize who God wants you to be and, practically, how to position yourself spiritually for success.

The teachings are clear and will strengthen you in your relationship and trust in the Eternal being, and you can become more Christ-like, as you read and pray.

This new book will cause you to authentically become a spiritual warrior with a deeper intimacy and love for God and others. In the fullness of time, and pursuing life and establishing God's dreams for us, it's a very powerful and profound read. As an eternal optimist interceding for my nation and existing in an inward state of quiet hope, this book came at the right time to encourage me. It will help you, too. Get the series!

Julie Anderson
Prayer for the Nations
London, England

MANIFESTING YOUR SPIRIT

GRAHAM COOKE

BOOK 2 THE WAY OF THE WARRIOR SERIES

www.BrilliantBookHouse.com

Brilliant
BOOK HOUSE

Unless otherwise indicated, all Scripture quotations are taken from The Holy Bible, New King James Version (Copyright © 1979, 1980, 1982 by Thomas Nelson, Inc.) and the New American Standard Bible (Copyright © 1960, 1962, 1963, 1971, 1972, 1973, 1975, 1977, 1995 by The Lockman Foundation).

Please note that Brilliant Book House has made the stylistic choice to capitalize certain words and pronouns that refer to the Father, Son and Holy Spirit, although it may differ from the stylistic choices of other publishers.

Manifesting Your Spirit, 1st edition ©2008

BRILLIANT BOOK HOUSE
PO BOX 871450
Vancouver, WA, 98687

This book and all other materials published by Graham Cooke are available online at BrilliantBookHouse.com

If you would like more information on Graham Cooke and his ministry, please visit GrahamCooke.com

ISBN 978-0-9896262-1-7

DEDICATION

I dedicate this book to my great friend and mentor, Jim McNeish, and the House of Cantle, which is his dream in Jesus come true.

I miss the times when Jim, Tony, Billy, Caroline, and I would spend days together eating, laughing, exploring Jesus in new ways. I loved the beyond-the-box thinking, the journey into mystery, searching afresh the deeper spirituality in the Word and the Spirit.

It's where I learned that I could love God with my mind as well as my heart, soul, and physical strength. I love having brilliant thoughts about God, and I adore turning that thinking onto the lives of people around me.

There is no doubt that believing the best has gotten me into a lot of trouble, mostly with cynical, judgmental, and offended people. However, not believing the best makes our journey into Christ more arduous. It keeps the flesh preserved and opens up huge tracts of negativity in our personality.

Life is too precious to condone negativity.

ACKNOWLEDGEMENTS

The Tribe

Since I first began speaking in the early 1970s there have been an increasing number of people who have collected my works, supported the ministry and massively encouraged me on this journey to the present day.

They are the people who share their story and journey, and testify of the life changes they have seen in themselves and their church as a result of reading or listening to my materials.

They are the first to book into particular events, the first to get the latest resource material, the first to let me know the fresh impact of new products. They are our Tribe, members of our company from all walks of life, all denominations, and all over the globe. They pray for us, dream about us, walk with us, and tell their friends what God is doing through us.

They are Brilliant. Our tribe, our people, our company. Committed to living from Heaven to Earth; thinking brilliantly, having a perspective and language based on the new man in Christ. They are growing in their identity, overcoming negativity, and learning the ways of God.

All my material is written with them in mind. Brilliant Book House, Brilliant Perspectives, and the Tribe.

Together we are all Team Brilliant.

INVOCATION

Father, thank you for the life-giving water that resides in each of us. You are a well and a fountain. We declare that we do not thirst except for a deeper walk with You.

Dig out that inner well, O Lord, so that hundreds may drink from what you pour out in us. Teach us to be resilient, passionate, and alive!

Infuse us with your exuberance till we are massively encouraged—constantly. Develop the internal place of our heart so that it becomes Your living space.

Empower us, great God, to see life exactly as You do—to view everything and everyone through the lens of Jesus. Teach us to think with the mind of Christ so that our thoughts are an extension of our worship.

As You manifest Your Spirit to us, may the privilege of our encounters with You release the hearts of many to come further on and further in.

For Jesus' sake.
Amen.

CONTENTS

WAKING UP YOUR INNER MAN

There is an activation I like to do in certain events that really develops the muscles of faith by rejoicing. Whenever we are developing people for life in the spirit or preparing them for battle, confidence and boldness must always be part of the training.

Note: Read this activation through twice before you do it. Do it with all the strength and passion you can generate.

I invite them to come to the front of the room and line up, shoulder to shoulder, in rows, as an army in formation would stand. I ask them to close their eyes and imagine that they are on a battlefield, and then I lead them through the following meditation:

Imagine that you are on a battlefield. Your army is small, especially in the face of the massive force that opposes you. You're outnumbered. You're outgunned. They're bigger than you in both number and physical size. A thought flashes across your mind: you're going to die. With everything stacked against you, you realize your only hope of survival is to run away. But you are a warrior: retreat is not an option.

In your heart, you decide you will fight as best you can. If you're going down, you're taking as many of them down with you as possible. You feel your face turn to flint as you prepare yourself. The resolve inside of you turns your blood cold. You push any fear out of your body: you don't need it; you don't want it. The butterflies in your stomach are now frozen in the concrete of your resolve. You turn your gaze onto the tallest, meanest-looking enemy you can see. That's the one you're going to kill first.

Now look eighteen inches above that enemy soldier. Do you see who's there? It's Jesus, grinning and waving at you. When you make eye contact with Him, He winks. The enemy has no clue that He's there — it's a private joke between Him and you. The Lord flips you a thumbs-up. "He's really going to enjoy this," you think to yourself. In your spirit, your resolve is joined by boldness and faith. Everything is different now because the King is here. This is going to be a good fight, because you're going to overcome all odds and win.

In your inner being, with your mouth closed, look at Jesus and shout. Show it on your face, wave your hands if you wish, but stay quiet. Inside of you, shout His name. Praise Him! Every fiber of your being is shouting to Him. Continue to praise and rejoice until every part of you is shouting and cheering on the inside. Let every part of your own caution, negativity, and fear dissolve in the face of His Majesty!

Now look again at the enemy army. See how confused they look? Their weak, timid, outnumbered enemy has been infused with confidence. They're now the ones who are worried. What are you up to?

*When you looked at Jesus' face, you proclaimed His goodness.
Now, looking at the enemy, I want you to declare what Jesus
will do to them. They're toast. It's over. The name of Jesus
will be victorious no matter what they try. The King is here!*

Begin shouting towards the enemy using your inner voice.
(Continue to keep your mouth closed.) Shout out his demise.
He is powerless! Jesus has defeated him! The battle is the
Lord's; the victory is ours! The Cross has overthrown his
power to rule. He is a conquered enemy.

The Lord has vanquished him. We are overcomers by the
Word of the Lord and the blood of His testimony.

Shout! Shout! Shout out his defeat, until every part of
you is on fire with passion for the battle. You cannot lose
because Jesus has already conquered.

Now, look at the enemy. See the fear in their eyes. See
their confusion, their questioning when they look at you.
You seem bigger to them, stronger, bolder, more powerful.
When they look at you they are staring defeat in the face.

How does that feel to you? What happened on the inside
of you? If you really participated in this exercise fully, something has changed. What is it? What woke up on the inside
of you? Journal your thoughts and feelings.

*This army exercise, allows us to go straight
to the inner man of the spirit.*

3

PERSONAL NOTES

DIGGING
OUT A WELL

Manifesting your spirit is a spiritual discipline, one explained by Jesus Himself in John 7:37–39:

Jesus stood and cried out, saying, "If anyone thirsts, let him come to Me and drink. He who believes in Me, as the Scripture has said, out of his heart will flow rivers of living water." But this He spoke concerning the Spirit, whom those believing in Him would receive; for the Holy Spirit was not yet given, because Jesus was not yet glorified.

Jesus also talked about this experience in John 4:14: "But whoever drinks of the water that I shall give him will never thirst. But the water that I shall give him will become in him a fountain of water springing up into everlasting life."

Life in the Spirit is about digging out a well. God wants to dig into us, removing the dirt and things that cover up the living water He has put within us. It is simple displacement—there are things that He must remove in order for the Holy Spirit to completely fill us. The Lord has to take out of us what shouldn't be there so that He can put in what

He wants to give us. Displacement ensures that the Holy Spirit has enough room inside of us to move and accomplish what He wants to accomplish.

Opposition attaches to what we don't remove. We give the enemy certain rights over our lives when we fail to partner with the Lord in our ongoing development. As in the world, water is of crucial importance. In some countries it is power. Water gives life. There can be no quality of life without it. Water is currency. In some nations those who control the water supply get wealth.

Similarly, in the spirit, those who develop their inner well, have power over life and the enemy. When we maintain our well, we are always refreshed. We do not get tired; our bodies are stronger. We are more mentally renewed, and our emotions are balanced. Life in the Spirit is a refreshing journey. We stay fresher, longer. We do not get beaten down, defeated, or dried out.

Too many Christians are dehydrated spiritually. We are prone to dejection, depression, and despondency—too easily downcast, with a negative mindset, and overly cautious. These are the spiritual signs of someone who is not processing the life of Jesus properly.

Rejoicing, praise, and thanksgiving keep us hydrated and in confidence. There is only one way to live this life, and that is the way that Jesus lives it! Dig out your well, maintain it properly, and drink the water—all day, every day. Take deliberate drinks of the Holy Spirit at specific times and in particular situations.

Digging out a well is about the precise act of displacement: taking out a negative by exposing it to the goodness and kindness of God, and replacing it with one of His own attributes—love instead of fear, trust instead of anxiety, faith instead of doubt, a garland instead of ashes, the oil of gladness instead of mourning, and a mantle of praise instead of a spirit of despair.

Water creates life. The Holy Spirit generates power. Maintain a great relationship with God through the Holy Spirit. He is a wonderful companion. He is wise, gentle, exuberant, excited by life, and totally enthusiastic about us. He is powerful, funny, and delightful. He adores Jesus and loves to reveal Him to us. He loves us incredibly and has incredible esteem in His heart towards us. He is a genius at everything! He is particularly brilliant at establishing the life of Christ in our experience.

Maintaining our inner well properly is mostly concerned with developing our personal relationship with the Holy Spirit. He is a person, not a force. He has a fabulous personality, just like the Father and Jesus. He helps us with everything. We are in the business of getting to know Him, working with Him, and listening to Him. We get to know the Father intimately through the Holy Spirit's relationship with Him. We fully embrace the sovereignty and majesty of Jesus in our lifestyle through the Holy Spirit's deep love for Him.

We rely on the Holy Spirit. He is our come-alongside friend, our personal tutor who trains us for every eventuality and for all aspects of life. Even when we are going through

7

a necessary wilderness experience, it is the Holy Spirit who gives us water, through our own internal well.

ASSIGNMENT

🦁 What are you going through at this time? What is the Lord displacing in you? What is He extracting that is worthless, and what is His precious replacement? How will the Holy Spirit help you with that? Don't just say, "I don't know." Ask Him! Wait around for the answer. Learn how to partner with Him.

COMMISSION

🦁 Take your relationship with the Holy Spirit to the next level of God's intention. Clean out your well. Make sure you are rehydrated. Ask the Father to restore your energy. Joy is infectious and cannot be denied. What needs to grow in relationship between you and the Holy Spirit? Read John 4:14 and 7:37–39 again. What do the promises mean to you? How will their daily fulfillment change your lifestyle of spirituality? What must change for that to be accomplished?

PERSONAL NOTES

INTERNAL FRAME
OF REFERENCE

T*oo many Christians have no* frame of reference for God. They have no internal, personalized experience or expression of God's presence. Their experience is mostly physical and mental, or what is called soulish in nature. Because it is physical and mental, it depends on physical and mental stimuli to exist. But the spirit is so much more than that. This is why I walk people through the army exercise—it allows them to go straight to the inner man of the spirit.

Spiritual warriors internalize their relationships with God. Put simply, they live from within. They know that power flows from the inside to the outside, not the other way around. God has already put inside every Christian something that needs to be manifested. It must be revealed, declared, and exposed. That's why the Holy Spirit is constantly seeking to cause our inner man of the spirit to rise up and manifest itself in the course of everyday life.

Everything we need will be made real as we exercise faith and dependence on the Lord. The word manifest means to show or demonstrate plainly. In the spiritual sense, it means to become a literal sign of God's revelation.

When I use the army exercise with a group, things change in the room. Many people get physically into the role of a warrior. Their faces change, their postures change. They begin to scowl and then grin confidently. Some stand taller. Others clench their fists and grit their teeth.

I love that exercise. It always starts the same way, with people uncomfortable and nervous. They laugh with each other and bump one another. But once we start the exercise of manifesting the will, it all changes. Something comes over them—or, more accurately, something flows out of them. They become a sign of the revelation God has put inside them.

Having an internal frame of reference means that in any given situation we do not take our truth from external circumstances. The world always gives us negative information. We ask the Father for His perspective.

We never ask, "Why?" It is the wrong question. It is an invalid question that makes us an invalid. It is a victim question, and the Father never makes us victims. He trains us to fight, to overcome, and to be more than conquerors in Christ. If the Father has never been overwhelmed, and Jesus is undefeated, then the Holy Spirit can only lead us in triumph.

An internal frame of reference takes all its testimonies from the Godhead. We learn to perceive in the spirit. Wisdom is the understanding of how God thinks, how He sees things, and how He likes to act in a given situation.

The two best questions we can ask in every life event are both spoken on the day of Pentecost: "What does this mean?" and "What shall we do?" [Acts 2:12; 2:37]. In between those two questions comes a whole wealth of revelation and an experience of God to go with it.

An internal frame of reference creates the space in us to discover God in the midst of any life event. It empowers us to look forward and anticipate. It enables us to look back in hindsight and determine anything that we may have missed, so that we complete our learning circle in terms of present, future, and past. The Lord goes before us, so we can anticipate. He walks with us so that we are aware of His present intention. He comes behind us so that we can ascertain what we could also have learned.

Anticipation, awareness, and ascertaining are critical forms of developing wisdom in our walk with God. I use my internal frame of reference not only for specific situations, but on a daily basis as a lifestyle relationship. I love to know, and God loves to talk… perfect.

So many times we go into situations blind and unprepared. God gave us eyes to see and ears to hear in the spirit. Jesus was always knowing, especially in the invisible. He knew what was in the hearts of men so he was never caught off guard by trick questions from religiously intolerant people. He knew when virtue went out of Him as the woman with the issue of blood touched Him in a crowd. He knew the best time to visit Lazarus was when all natural hope was gone.

He knew how to wait on His Father, how to commune with the Holy Spirit, and how to live from the inside-out. If you have ever taken a walk through dense woodland, without any path, you will know how hard it is to walk without any real bearings. The journey is hard: we never walk in a straight line; we are constantly navigating trees, bushes, and overgrowth. When we do eventually come into a clearing, we step into the middle and stop! We look at the heavens, we look around, and we take a breath—time to reorient and reorder ourselves. That is exactly what we do regarding our internal frame of reference. We take time to stop and listen. We ask God's perspective: we seek wisdom, not knowledge. "Father, what does this mean?" It's a fabulous question! We never assume. Our starting point for revelation is always with the Father, never the situation. We do not live in our circumstances: we live in Christ. Therefore, it is His opinion that is most desirable.

Our circumstances are not the problem. It is our perception of the circumstances that is the problem. To Gideon, losing 99% of his army was definitely a problem on one level, but not if God had a specific purpose for the 300 who remained! Sometimes God is such a genius He uses the enemy to encourage us and develop our frame of reference, as in this instance in Judges 7:9–15:

Now the same night it came about that the Lord said to him, "Arise, go down against the camp, for I have given it into your hands. But if you are afraid to go down, go with Purah your servant down to the camp, and you will hear what they say; and afterward your hands will be strengthened that you may go down against the camp." So he went with Purah his servant down to the outposts of the army that was in the camp.

Now the Midianites and the Amalekites and all the sons of the east were lying in the valley as numerous as locusts; and their camels were without number, as numerous as the sand on the seashore.

When Gideon came, behold, a man was relating a dream to his friend. And he said, "Behold, I had a dream; a loaf of barley bread was tumbling into the camp of Midian, and it came to the tent and struck it so that it fell, and turned it upside down so that the tent lay flat."

His friend replied, "This is nothing less than the sword of Gideon the son of Joash, a man of Israel; God has given Midian and all the camp into his hand."

When Gideon heard the account of the dream and its interpretation, he bowed in worship. He returned to the camp of Israel and said, "Arise, for the Lord has given the camp of Midian into your hands."

Gideon is made aware of God's current plan and develops anticipation of the outcome. He is immeasurably strengthened. He is still outnumbered by 400 to 1 and there is much to be done, but he has outstanding assurance. That is what an internal frame of reference accomplishes. It takes all the wisdom and perception of God and re-orients us so that we are perfectly positioned to take advantage of the external situation around us.

It is our privilege to live this way consistently. "As He is so are we in this world," [1 John 4:17]. We have the mind of Christ. Developing an internal frame of reference is a part of our partnership with the Holy Spirit in "being renewed in the Spirit of our mind" [Ephesians 4:23].

All our life transformations come from a renewed mindset. Circumstances are transformed when we think differently about them. Now we discover that far from a situation being against us, it can actually be designed to work for us!

We can have a frame of reference that creates a negative disposition. It is what Paul viewed as a mind set on the flesh. Romans 8:5–8:

> *For those who are according to the flesh set their minds on the things of the flesh, but those who are according to the Spirit, the things of the Spirit.*
>
> *For the mind set on the flesh is death, but the mind set on the Spirit is life and peace, because the mind set on the flesh is hostile toward God; for it does not subject itself to the law of God, for it is not even able to do so, and those who are in the flesh cannot please God.*

When we view life from a place outside of who God is for us we take on board a perspective that is hostile to the purpose of the Father. We cannot cooperate with Him nor partner with people around us. When our thinking is hostile to heavenly purpose it is reflected in our lack of peace and an impoverished lifestyle. Repentance is the art of thinking again, so that our actions are governed from a better place of thought.

If all of our thinking has brought us to a place that we do not like, then surely it is time for us to have another thought!

ASSIGNMENT

🦁 In your present circumstances, have you been captured by a negative viewpoint? Has your thinking taken you to a place of peace and purpose? What needs to change in you?

🦁 What would transformation look like for you in your present circumstances? What is the necessary line of thought that could restore you to peace and purpose?

COMMISSION

🦁 Check out your present thoughts and attitudes towards God, yourself, others, and current circumstances. What is working well, and why is that so? What is clearly not working, and what is the impact of that on yourself and your relationships? How cautious, fearful, and negative are you about life in general?

🦁 Submit yourself to a check up, using the Holy Spirit and other people. Give yourself a tune up in terms of faith and positivity. Your life may resemble a car that badly needs service. Failure to adjust guarantees a breakdown later.

🦁 If you are already broken down, it is your thinking that has wrecked you. You must take some time out to take those negative, cynical thoughts captive. They are corroding your heart relationships and denying you the joy of life in Christ. A time out now to correct this imbalance is absolutely vital. Take some honest feedback from others. It cannot hurt you more than you are already hurting yourself. It's time to get healed.

PERSONAL NOTES

TO MANIFEST
MEANS TO
MAKE VISIBLE

Manifestation of the spirit occurs when we are God-conscious, that is, when we are more aware of Him than we are of ourselves. When we understand that everything we need to succeed spiritually is already inside of us, we become fully focused on letting God do His work. We can draw out of that provision like a thirsty man draws water from a well. We pull the bucket up by using our faith, confession, proclamation, worship, praise, witness, and declaration.

Our spirit man is linked to our vocal chords. Watching people do the exercise, I always marvel at how many cannot stay quiet. Most people long to shout to Jesus, and get frustrated when they aren't allowed to. That inner man of the spirit needs a voice; it needs to be spoken out loud. We see over and over in Scripture that God acts when we shout:

"The LORD their God is with them; the shout of the King is among them" [Numbers 23:21].

"Grasping the torches in their left hands and holding in their right hands the trumpets they were to blow, they shouted, 'A sword for the LORD and for Gideon!'" [Judges 7:20]

"When the ark of the LORD's covenant came into the camp, all Israel raised such a great shout that the ground shook" [1 Samuel 4:5].

"So all Israel brought up the ark of the covenant of the LORD with shouts" [1 Chronicles 15:28].

"They took an oath to the LORD with loud acclamation, with shouting and with trumpets and horns" [2 Chronicles 15:14].

"Sing to him a new song; play skillfully, and shout for joy" [Psalm 33:3].

"Clap your hands, all you nations; shout to God with cries of joy" [Psalm 47:1].

"God has ascended amid shouts of joy, the LORD amid the sounding of trumpets" [Psalm 47:5].

"Shout aloud and sing for joy, people of Zion, for great is the Holy One of Israel among you" [Isaiah 12:6].

"The crowds that went ahead of him and those that followed shouted, 'Hosanna to the Son of David!' 'Blessed is he who comes in the name of the Lord!' 'Hosanna in the highest!'" [Matthew 21:9]

We must connect verbally to fully manifest our spirit. The greatest Scriptural example of this principle can be found in Joshua 6, when God gave the heavily fortified city of Jericho to the Israelites after they literally shouted down its mighty walls. For six days, every Hebrew man, woman, and child had walked silently around the city. On the seventh day, they walked around the city six more times, before

Joshua declared God's plan: "And the seventh time it happened, when the priests blew the trumpets, that Joshua said to the people: 'Shout, for the LORD has given you the city!'" [Joshua 6:16]

When faced with an impenetrable obstacle, ordinary solutions will not work. We should all appreciate that God is not a conventional thinker. He is not conservative in His actions. He thinks not just outside the box, but beyond it! He is not subject to logic or reason. He is much too clever to be an intellectual. His thinking transcends the normal intelligence of man. It is spiritual, wise, creative, and full of imagination.

To partake of His strategies, we must fully engage with the whole person. We dare not leave anything out, in terms of our response. If our response is not wholehearted, we will lose or only get a partial victory. Our ability to overcome is tied to the level of our response. There is a perfect example of this in 2 Kings 13:14–19:

> *When Elisha became sick with the illness of which he was to die, Joash the king of Israel came down to him and wept over him and said, "My father, my father, the chariots of Israel and its horsemen!"*
>
> *Elisha said to him, "Take a bow and arrows." So he took a bow and arrows.*
>
> *Then he said to the king of Israel, "Put your hand on the bow." And he put his hand on it, then Elisha laid his hands on the king's hands.*
>
> *He said, "Open the window toward the east," and he opened it. Then Elisha said, "Shoot!" And he shot. And he said, "The Lord's arrow of victory, even the arrow of victory over Aram;*

*for you will defeat the Arameans at Aphek until you have
destroyed them."*

*Then he said, "Take the arrows," and he took them. And he
said to the king of Israel, "Strike the ground," and he struck
it three times and stopped.*

*So the man of God was angry with him and said, "You should
have struck five or six times, then you would have struck
Aram until you would have destroyed it. But now you shall
strike Aram only three times."*

An improper response achieves a poor result. How do
you imagine Joash felt on the morning of the fourth battle?
We get opportunities in life to break through into a place of
overwhelming victory. The enemy can prevent the victory,
and he can also downsize it. It is our wholehearted response
that makes us more than conquerors. It means that we do
not just win the fight; we occupy the territory afterwards.
God had a plan for Jericho that was not found in any conventional military strategy.

God's plan worked perfectly, as it always does.

*"So the people shouted when the priests blew the trumpets. And
it happened when the people heard the sound of the trumpet,
and the people shouted with a great shout, that the wall fell
down flat. Then the people went up into the city, every man
straight before him, and they took the city." [Joshua 6:20]*

Manifestation involves the whole person. Body, mind,
emotion, and spirit must all act in agreement. The Israelites
walked in silent agreement for seven days. It probably took
that long to still all of their minds and focus them on what

God was about to do. When they had proved their unity, they spoke it out; and God manifested His plan.

To partner with God takes everything we are and have. There is no place for a lukewarm response. When we manifest our spirit, every part of us is in wholehearted agreement with God. To shout aloud is the ultimate response. To proclaim is the ultimate accolade.

It is the lack of proclamation in the church that has stripped us of our full response to the majesty of Jesus. Not only are individuals not taught to proclaim in respect of their own life events, there is also no place in our worship or prayer life corporately for us to experience declarative announcements. Majesty requires proclamation. It is a necessity—not a luxury. It is a staple part of our warfare. We are heralds of the King.

Manifesting our inner man of the spirit releases power. It positions us before God—not just the enemy. We manifest our spirit in worship first. That is, we call up all that we are in Christ for the sake of true worship and adoration. We are replenished by our passion. Lukewarm worship produces nothing. We are still tired, weary, and oppressed by circumstances. Full engagement in worship lifts us above the battle and the heads of our enemies. Proclamation rejuvenates us. Faith rises naturally. Joy is restored fully. We have energy because we have Presence!

ASSIGNMENT

✦ To manifest means to make visible. Do the people around you know what your inner man sounds like? Have they heard your inner man in worship? Have they seen you proclaim? Do they know the sound of full engagement with God?

✦ We need to know the sound of our own warfare. Overcoming is not a silent movie. The sound of it is loud. Everyone makes a sound, raises a shout—introverts and extroverts, the same! Everyone has to meditate on God—introverts and extroverts, the same!

✦ Your inner man has access to all the personality of God. We are not handicapped by our introversion or our extroversion. We have no excuse and no valid reason for not manifesting our inner man.

✦ Get to know your inner sound. Pray aloud, read aloud, sing out loud. Rejoice. Give thanks with a loud voice. Shout to the Lord. Get beyond your personality. Crucially, get above your embarrassment. Do not allow it to drag you down.

✦ Discover your level of embarrassment and determine to overcome yourself. Remember, this is not logical; it's spiritual. Your inner man has to be fully awake and seen in action. To manifest means to make visible.

COMMISSION

🐉 Create a dialogue with some friends. Share your thoughts and concerns about your personal lack of proclamation. Pray together. Create an opportunity in your circumstances for all of you to come to a place of worship and proclamation. Do it. Activate your inner man. Collectively, overcome embarrassment; experience God's personality. Practice. Practice until something changes in you, or you experience a breakthrough in your circumstances.

PERSONAL NOTES

PERSONAL NOTES

AGREE WITH
YOUR TRAINER!

Most *believers do not practice agreement* between themselves and the work of the Holy Spirit. They can be soulish, led mostly by their feelings, and heavily influenced by rational thinking. They do not live by the spirit because they usually use logic to talk themselves out of the spiritual dimension.

So true!

But God rarely employs a logical plan. Often, He tells us things that simply do not make rational sense. While it resonates with the inner man of our spirit, it offends the soulish nature of our own mind. Our brain then spends the next few minutes talking us out of the plan.

Spiritual warriors know that God's plans are not like ours. They are often illogical, implausible, and sometimes completely impossible! Who else but God would send thousands of people walking around a city for six days in complete silence? Who else but God would conceive of a plan to bring a wall down by shouting at it? You and I would have built catapults, ramps, ladders, and battering rams. God used some vocal chords. If I gave you a prophecy to walk around a city for seven days, shout, and watch the walls tumble down, you would have me committed. Things that God says supernaturally will not always make sense to our logical minds.

When we each first heard the Gospel, it didn't make complete sense to us. Yet something started to work inside of us; and whether it made sense or not, we knew we needed it. That was God digging through the mire covering our spirit so we could feel His touch again.

To reduce the experience of God to either an intellectual or emotional process is to deny His power and make it impossible to receive His Presence. In our relationship with the Holy Spirit, we are learning a language of faith. We are mastering the ability to see through a wholly different lens. God's perceptions are Heaven-sent; that is, they originate in Heaven and come to Earth. It is a viewpoint from a higher place and a totally different dimension.

Clearly, if we are to walk with the Father in His ways, then our earthbound thinking requires serious adjustment. He lives in the "all things are possible" realm. We live in a place of seeming impossibility. In His universe, limbs can grow back; sight can be restored along with hearing and speech; internal organs can reappear as new; and all manner of sickness, mental confusion, and emotional disorder can be fully healed.

In His realm, His abundance in Heaven obliterates our poverty on Earth. In His domain, we are never outclassed, overwhelmed, or overcome. No matter what is against us, we can win through His name. Impossible odds are fun to Him, who loves to laugh at His enemies.

We are learning how to occupy a seat in heavenly places in Christ, so that His viewpoint of our circumstances is the one that dominates our thinking, praying, and believing. We are disciples of another realm, learning the lessons of abiding in Christ so that what is in Heaven may come to Earth through our relationship with the Holy Spirit.

He is our tutor from Heaven. He is given to teach us the ways of Heaven and Earth. Through Him we learn that whatever has been bound in Heaven may also be bound on Earth. Whatever Heaven is releasing may also be loosed on Earth. These are known as the keys of the kingdom [Matthew 16:19]. What is not tolerated in Heaven cannot be condoned on Earth.

"Your kingdom come, Your will be done, on earth as it is in heaven," [Matthew 6:10] is a significant part of the Lord's prayer. The same kingdom must be established on Earth that abides in Heaven. We are citizens of Heaven, while living here on Earth [Philippians 3:20, Ephesians 2:19]. In that place of being raised up with Christ, we seek only the things of Heaven, where Christ is seated at God's right hand [Colossians 3:1].

We are discipled by the Holy Spirit to learn to live from another dimension. He is training us to bring Heaven to Earth by our prayers, faith, and obedience. There are, therefore, important and significant lessons to be learned, if we are to be commissioned from on high.

To learn effectively, we must agree with our tutor—not supply Him with our unbelieving curriculum. He has no theology of powerlessness. It is complete nonsense to say that we have a tutor assigned to us from Heaven, but He can only teach us to be earthbound in our thinking and believing. The Holy Spirit sets us free in Christ to do greater things than He did, which was one of His extravagant promises to us.

To live in the flow of God's outpouring, we must drink in the culture of Heaven and adopt all of its character and ways. To do that best we must love our tutor. Spending time with Him must become one of our highest pleasures. Attaining the lifestyle of Heaven must be a joyful experience. Watching the impossible become possible is part of a normal Christian life.

ASSIGNMENT

🦁 How much of your thinking is earthbound in logic and rational thought? What does the phrase "we have the mind of Christ" actually mean to your life? What agreements do you need to make with the Holy Spirit in order to be discipled from Heaven?

COMMISSION

🦁 How will you position yourself before God so that "on earth as it is in heaven" can be your usual experience? What are the ways that you need to "abide in Christ" in this present season? What are you learning about the language of faith and seeing in the spirit?

PERSONAL NOTES

PERSONAL NOTES

THE STARTING POINT FOR BREAKTHROUGH

The *starting point for spiritual* breakthrough lies in the will. Spiritual discipline is the process of submitting our will to the desires of the inner man of the spirit. Our spirits can only rule over our body and soul through an act of our will. The will is the vehicle that God uses to establish faith and govern our minds and emotions. We must turn our will over to God in order to live in the spirit constantly.

"It is God who works in you both to will and to do for His good pleasure," says Philippians 2:13. Before God can do anything with us, He has to get a hold of our will. If someone refuses to put their will under the rule of God, He will not do anything. It is the will that acts on the mind and that forms attitude and approach. Our feelings follow in the same way our will engages.

It is sometimes difficult for Christians to understand that our will is cold-blooded. It should be very rarely emotionally influenced. We can make a cold-blooded, unemotional decision to do something, and our faith will rise. If you are searching for some kind of emotional context in order to feel like doing something, it will never happen. Your will does not need your emotions to function. Obviously, they can and will combine, but it has to be under your will's direction and rule. Your emotions cannot be allowed to rule you.

A spiritual warrior allows God to re-direct his will. Warriors struggle with it. Most are willful, resolute, steadfast people, so it is only natural that this would be a difficult choice to make. But they do make that choice, and they do submit their will to God.

God works on the will first, and then through it, He renews the mind, gets a hold of our emotions, and transforms us. As that transformation happens, our faith rises. God gave us a will so that we would never be at the mercy of our emotions, which are influenced by so many different things. Spiritual warriors are willing to allow God to touch them, believing He is doing it even when they don't feel it. "God says it, I believe it, and that jolly well settles it." Sometimes faith is just that cold-blooded.

God loves our emotions, but He has created a context, a divine order, in which they may be experienced. That order is that the will is paramount in our approach to God and believing. The will adores God and is designed to receive Him. God works in the will in order to upgrade faith.

As faith arises, we worship, trust, and obey. Once faith is present, we can be transformed in our thinking to experience who God is for us. Feelings can come to the party, but they cannot organize it. Breakthrough is an act of the will.

34

Sometimes the will may use our emotions, at other times our thinking is given an upgrade. There are also times when the will goes it alone with God, and we do things that don't make sense and make us nervous. There is plenty of precedent here in Scripture with Abraham, Moses, Gideon, Joshua, David, Peter, and Paul. All had immense challenges, impossible circumstances, and faced overwhelming odds; yet they found the Lord to be real, true, and powerful. They overcame. They knew that the starting point for breakthrough is always in the will.

Any thought or emotion not centered in the will is going to talk us out of faith into logic. The development of our will as a key source of anointing is one of the major disciplines in our relationship with God.

Discipline is about enjoyment. It is concerned with loving the learning that is present in all situations. Love your trainer! You will learn better and faster.

ASSIGNMENT

What breakthrough do you need at this time? What has prevented you from receiving it before now? What adjustment must you make in your will in this situation? What is the learning that you must love, so that you may successfully overcome?

COMMISSION

Read or re-read *Towards A Powerful Inner Life*[1] and complete the assignments.

---

1   Available at www.BrilliantBookHouse.com

PERSONAL NOTES

FAITH'S PARTNERSHIP WITH THE WILL

Because faith and will both depend on God's truth, when put together, they are enough to create a move of God in our spirit. An act of will can set recovery in motion. The key is to continually remind ourselves what is true about the nature of God.

I am constantly awed by the kindness of God in my life. That's why I mention it in every sermon I preach and every book I write. His kindness is just too real for me to ignore. This is my truth about God: He has been relentlessly kind to me for many years. I am now completely dependent upon that kindness, and I work to represent that gift to everyone I meet. God wants us to be a testimony of His nature. When people look at us, they should see something of God. When people look at me, I want them to see God's kindness.

What is true for you about the power of the Holy Spirit? Who is God to you that you can show the world? What specific victory did Christ buy for you personally? We know that in general terms the Lord bought victory for all of our life.

However, there are specific areas of bondage, oppression and difficulty in which the Lord Jesus has especially set us free, so that we may deliver others in His name.

Our individual understanding of God's nature is the central point of our confession. That confession, combined with our will, keeps us standing when we feel like falling. Supplication becomes declaration when we engage our will. We move from "Lord, don't let me fall," to "Lord, we will not fall." Prayers begging God to do something transform into proclamations that He will do it.

In the army exercise I used at the beginning of this book, I have found that most Christians feel a sense of supplication in those early moments before they see Jesus. The enemy is so large and seemingly unbeatable that they cannot help but beg God for help. While there is nothing wrong with supplication in moments of crisis, spiritual warriors see a fight like that in a different light. They see it not as a crisis, but as an opportunity for greatness. A spiritual warrior looks at an army like that and declares the truth: "God is about to defeat you." The vision of a conquering Christ that is stitched into their hearts transforms everything they see. They do not have to do an exercise to see Jesus grinning at them—they have been living under the glory of that smile their entire lives.

This is the attitude that made Caleb a "man of a different spirit" in the eyes of God. He took his perspectives from Heaven. He was a man of intimacy as well as a man of action.

He alone opposed the report of the unbelieving spies and stood against the criticism of Moses' leadership. Numbers 13:30:

Then Caleb quieted the people before Moses and said, "We should by all means go up and take possession of it, for we will surely overcome it."

The next day Joshua joined Caleb and in the face of incredible opposition and unbelief spoke out of the combination of the will and faith. Numbers 14:4–10:

So they said to one another, "Let us appoint a leader and return to Egypt."

Then Moses and Aaron fell on their faces in the presence of all the assembly of the congregation of the sons of Israel.

Joshua the son of Nun and Caleb the son of Jephunneh, of those who had spied out the land, tore their clothes;

and they spoke to all the congregation of the sons of Israel, saying, "The land which we passed through to spy out is an exceedingly good land.

"If the LORD is pleased with us, then He will bring us into this land and give it to us—a land which flows with milk and honey.

"Only do not rebel against the LORD; and do not fear the people of the land, for they will be our prey. Their protection has been removed from them, and the LORD is with us; do not fear them."

But all the congregation said to stone them with stones. Then the glory of the LORD appeared in the tent of meeting to all the sons of Israel.

Glory attaches itself to faith and the will. When we are faced with overwhelming odds, and circumstances look impossible; faith and the will combined will see us through to a place where God may shine upon us. Faith and the will focus on who God is for us now! Warriors know that as we please God, so our stock rises and His abundance flows. Without faith it is impossible to please God [Hebrews 11:6]; but just as importantly, warriors also know that "whoever believes in Him will never be disappointed" [Romans 10].

What is true about God is the central point of our confession. Your faith confession combined with your will makes you stand when you feel like falling. It is impossible for God to let us down. Faith is the designed method for us to receive all that He wants to give. It therefore follows that the acquisition and development of faith is of paramount importance to the Father. If that is true, then Christians acquiring doubt, leading to unbelief, is a major part of the tactics of the enemy in our lives.

We doubt because we do not trust. Our doubts tell the world that our relationship with the Lord needs an upgrade. Trust is a relational issue. Proverbs 3:5–6:

> *Trust in the Lord with all your heart, and do not lean on your own understanding.*
>
> *In all your ways acknowledge Him, and He will make your paths straight.*

Trust is a matter of the heart. If we do not trust, we will depend on our own logic and ways of understanding that are mostly a product of our world environment. As we express heartfelt trust it leads us quite naturally to accepting God's perspective on our circumstances, and that generates a positive confession.

It is when we admit God's purpose that we begin to recognize the signs of His presence. We easily fall into a place of instruction from the Holy Spirit that enables us to partner with the Lord for our freedom and benefit.

Trust moves us swiftly into faith, whereas the destination of doubt is unbelief. The effect of unbelief upon our relationship with God is vile and destructive. We must do all we can in partnership with the Holy Spirit to cultivate faith.

ASSIGNMENT

What is true for you about the nature of God? What aspect of the power of the Holy Spirit do you need to experience in your current season? What victory of Christ do you need to acquire in your present situation?

COMMISSION

Who are you in Jesus at this time? What part of His life do you need to inherit next? What promotion is the Father bringing to your identity? What is the next upgrade in your faith?

PERSONAL NOTES

WARRIORS HAVE A ROYAL PERSPECTIVE

David was a man who understood and was bolstered by the power of God. Even as a young man, he knew that no battle was impossible with God on his side. It is this courage that has made his stories famous, with his victory over Goliath in 1 Samuel 17 being the most notable.

Goliath looked at David and saw an easy win. "Am I a dog, that you come to me with sticks?" he taunted in verses 43 and 44. "Come to me, and I will give your flesh to the birds of the air and the beasts of the field!"

Goliath's intimidation fell on deaf ears, as David knew where the real power resided, as we read in verses 45–47:

> *Then David said to the Philistine, "You come to me with a sword, with a spear, and with a javelin. But I come to you in the name of the LORD of hosts, the God of the armies of Israel, whom you have defied. This day the LORD will deliver you into my hand, and I will strike you and take your head from you. And this day I will give the carcasses of the camp*

of the Philistines to the birds of the air and the wild beasts of the earth, that all the earth may know that there is a God in Israel. Then all this assembly shall know that the LORD does not save with sword and spear; for the battle is the LORD's, and He will give you into our hands."

Throughout his life, David spoke out of his will. When he decided on a course of action, he saw it through—no matter what. His psalms are full of willful choices to trust God. One need only look at Psalm 27:1–6 to get a full sense of the trust in God a spiritual warrior should have:

The LORD is my light and my salvation; Whom shall I fear? The LORD is the strength of my life; Of whom shall I be afraid?

When the wicked came against me to eat up my flesh, my enemies and foes, they stumbled and fell.

Though an army may encamp against me, my heart shall not fear; though war may rise against me, in this I will be confident.

One thing I have desired of the LORD, that will I seek: That I may dwell in the house of the LORD all the days of my life, to behold the beauty of the LORD, and to inquire in His temple.

For in the time of trouble He shall hide me in His pavilion; in the secret place of His tabernacle He shall hide me; He shall set me high upon a rock.

And now my head shall be lifted up above my enemies all around me; therefore I will offer sacrifices of joy in His tabernacle; I will sing, yes, I will sing praises to the LORD.

David was not worried about fights where the odds were stacked against him. He knew that with God, every battle was winnable. He lived a life of fearless trust in God. David wrote Psalm 27 while he lived among the Philistines because of the enmity of Saul. If ever there was a moment to doubt God, that was it. Yet David, even in his lowest moments, clung to his faith that the Lord was in control. While hiding from the insane King Saul, he wrote Psalm 57:7 — "My heart is steadfast, O God, my heart is steadfast; I will sing and give praise." David knew to put the first things first; that is, he knew to praise God in the midst of every issue.

We can learn a lot from David's steadfast faith in the majesty of God. In Psalm 9:1–2, David made four "I will" statements that every spiritual warrior must make:

I will praise You, O LORD, with my whole heart; I will tell of all Your marvelous works.

I will be glad and rejoice in You; I will sing praise to Your name, O Most High.

When a Christian breaks through the barrier of their emotions and wills themselves to live out these statements in every circumstance, they become a spiritual warrior. Sometimes the Lord leaves us in a problem until we hate it enough to get rid of it forever. Mostly Christians will get rid of a problem temporarily and then welcome it back later.

David lived *from* God, not *towards* Him. Therefore his thinking was directed at the problem not at the Lord. Similarly, we have the mind of Christ. That means that we are to embrace a way of thinking and believing that is rooted in our lifestyle. We always position ourselves in this manner. Warriors have a certain posture that they adopt towards problems and the enemy. They live the life!

Too many Christians are event driven in their spirituality. The quality of their rejoicing, thanksgiving, conversation, and prayer with the Father runs low in terms of a lifestyle. When things happen they then come to God mostly in fear, to complain, to ask "why me?" They do not grow in these times because they merely want them to be sorted out so they can get back to normal. In this instance normal is another word for mediocrity.

When we treat faith as an event dynamic, we never have enough. Faith is a lifestyle. It is a posture in the goodness of God. It is a position we take before the God of favor. Faith is an assurance in our hearts and minds. Faith is provoked by majesty. It is rooted in relationship. Faith has a royal perspective because it keeps company with the King.

A royal outlook comes from throne room living. Time spent with God in the course of life means that His way of thinking clothes us in the mindset of Heaven. If our lifestyle with God is not relational but formal, then we spend moments with Him; and we hope that something rubs off on us in the contact.

David meditated. He loved God with his heart and also with his mind. There are four ways to love God, and we must do them all. We love Him with our heart, mind, soul, and strength—that is, with the centrality of our personality in the inner man of the spirit: with our thinking, wondering, and mindset/approach to life; with our will totally engaged to

46

serve, stand, and discover; finally, with our physical strength in worship, work, warfare, and actual support for others.

This requires that we live in Christ fully towards the Father as a lifestyle. Then, when adversity and warfare present themselves, we live in Christ fully from the Father. We deal in His mindset. We approach difficulties from a royal perspective. The mind that is in Christ Jesus is fully ours. It is not an adopted one for the circumstance. An adopted situational mindset cannot see enough of the amazing possibilities that are present, because it is mostly intent on problem resolution. A royal mindset thinks of an advantage to be gained beyond the problem itself. It sees a bigger picture. David was always ready to see the whole counsel of God. That is one of the many reasons he was described as a man after God's heart.

ASSIGNMENT

🦁 Is your walk with God truly relational or mostly formal? In adversity do you live towards God or from Him? Do you have to get your mind into gear when a problem comes, or does your mindset allow you to anticipate life in a more faith-filled way?

COMMISSION

🦁 Is it time to readjust the place where you live before God? Develop a lifestyle of being in Christ before the Father. In your present circumstances what would a royal perspective tell you to do? What should your position and posture be in the throne room? If you were visiting your problem from God what would you tell it?

Journey your way into a new mindset.

PERSONAL NOTES

RESILIENCE

O*n this journey of life,* we have choices to make in terms of how we are going to show up. What will we reveal to others about God, and about our relationship with Him? We can choose, for example, optimism or discouragement. We can choose to become positive by using our will properly or to become negative through allowing malaise or simple laziness.

Discouragement creeps up on us, and we often fall into it before we even realize what is happening. This is the result of not actually living in the mind of Christ. Earthbound living is inherently pessimistic, and we must be on our guard at all times. In my own walk with the Lord, I am dedicated to remaining positive. It is better to say, "I am quietly hopeful," than it is to say "I'm really down right now."

This is more than a change of language, it is a change of outlook. I live in quiet hope which has become a solid buttress against the enemy. If the enemy cannot even overcome your low place, he has no chance against the rest of you! Quiet hope is the place where I set my feet to stand effectively in the course of life. I am not despondent because I choose joy as a vehicle for life and living. My capacity to rest in the Lord is founded on quiet hope. In Heaven's terminology, hope is always seen as a confident expectation. Faith is the beginning of trust which leads us to active hope.

Hope does not allow the enemy any place to lie to us. It allows no deception. It refuses a negative. Despondence and discouragement never get a foot in the door of our heart. It is a solid defense that opens us up to all that God has purposed. Hope believes implicitly in the nature of God.

From trust we enter hope, through rejoicing. We trust in who God is for us. We give thanks and position ourselves to receive His blessing, promise, and favor. When trust and hope combine, we become vulnerable to revelation. Trust and hope produce peace, which guards our heart and mind. We are not overwhelmed; we are positioning ourselves to overcome. In our trust we smile, worship, and give thanks. We hear God speak, and faith comes by hearing.

Faith is the capacity to step out without caution. Faith is the empowerment to step into an unsafe place (in the natural) because you have permission from the Lord to go there. Faith is not a risk, it is an assurance built on hope. It is a cycle. Faith leads to trust, which releases an experience that produces knowledge which develops hope… a confident expectation of God.

Resilience is living in the middle of that cycle. It is the ability to withstand any shock that comes our way. Rest and peace are the best shock absorbers on Earth. When things begin to go against us, we need to recover quickly and reposition ourselves in God. Resilience is about much more than recovery.

It is concerned with developing an unbeatable lifestyle. It is about resolve. It is the discipline to agree with God, abide in Him, and simply to overcome because we don't run. David was resilient. "My heart is fixed O God, my heart is fixed." Psalm 57 is a great dialogue about overcoming through resilience. Though everything is against David, he demonstrates faith, trust, and hope. The combination of these attributes makes him resolute in his respect and glory of God. He calls up the glory of God [Verse 8] because to him God's glory is the major issue.

Resilient people exalt the Lord through their lifestyle. They are not mindful of the enemy, evil people, or desperate circumstances. They are focused on who God is for them. They are aware of circumstances, but are too much in awe of God. Resilience, empowers us to live peacefully. It enables us to have such a place of rest that we ignore the enemy completely. Jesus said of his own experience, "the prince of this world has come, but he has nothing on me" [John 14:30]. David's version is to confess that he is steadfast.

To be resolute is the beginning of boldness. We live a life that is learning to abide in consistency. Our resistance to the enemy is built on our submission to the Lord. The enemy must flee from a resilient life, or he will lose more than he ever hoped to gain [James 4:7].

A resilient life makes the enemy cut his losses and run for cover. When we live in Christ, there is a natural contending against the enemy that occurs unconsciously through our lifestyle. Everything we do for God is automatically against the evil one. Though not specifically directed, it offends him, disturbs him, and makes him work that much harder. Warriors make life tough for the enemy. The Lord has infinite resources; the enemy is limited to Earth. The Lord has abundance; the enemy has a budget.

His main mode of operation is intimidation, hoping that Christians will not show up for the fight. Intimidation is a necessary budget item in Hell. A lying, deceiving spirit is dispatched to fool people into giving up. In this way, territory can be gained without expense being incurred.

Resilient warriors are more expensive to fight—not just because the enemy has to commit more resources to the battle, but also because he could lose more than he bargained for in the conflict. In order to overcome Elijah, the enemy had to commit huge resources of 450 prophets of Baal and 400 prophets of Asherah (Jezebel's people). 1 Kings 18 tells the story of Elijah initiating the conflict and the enemy losing the hearts of an entire nation. Resilient warriors have a boldness, determination, and unshakable quality when they step into the conflict. They want to inflict pain and confusion on the enemy.

When flying into Australia many years ago, I was aware of the warfare around the conference. Between landing on the runway and the plane arriving at the gate, I was afflicted with a mouth full of ulcers. It hurt to eat, drink, and breathe. Talking was difficult, so I talked more than usual. I prophesied more than normal, and I had healing meetings for anyone who was sick. I did not consider myself to have a healing ministry at that time, but I knew the principle that was present in this particular conflict: where the stress is, the anointing is always present. The attack was against my voice, so I had an anointing present on anything I said!

I saw more people healed in those meetings than at any time before or since. I had more words of knowledge and more faith to call out sickness because of the attack on my voice. Brilliant! Resilience receives stamina and strength from the nature of God. He is a great encourager. He loves to strengthen us. It is our joy to be like Him.

When we fail to understand the nature of the kingdom, we only have our church culture to sustain us. Drawing strength from people around us is good, but not the best. Jesus is our source for all of life; people are a bonus. When God resources through people, they are an exceptional gift to us. I have a number of people who are a part of God's provision for the ministry, and they are quite outstanding friends. However, I need to hear God for myself primarily, and people are His confirmation. Occasionally, of course, that works in reverse too, which is wonderful.

The Father is undaunted and amused by the enemy. He laughs at him. We shelter in the Father's conviction and steadfast confidence. Resilient people are intentional. They have a fixed purpose and the permission from God to go with it. To stand, having done everything we can do in partnership with God… is actually an enjoyable experience. The Father supplies us with His own armor so that we can stand firm against the schemes of the devil [Ephesians 6:10–17].

Resistance is inbuilt to a life of awe in the majesty of God. Warriors are resilient because they live in the strength of His might.

ASSIGNMENT

🦁 What steps do you need to take to avoid negativity? How much of your culture assists you in developing the right mindset and lifestyle before the Lord? What aspects of your own spiritual language needs to improve and develop?

🦁 In regard to hope, trust, and faith; what is the Lord upgrading for you in these areas?

COMMISSION

🦁 Take steps to ensure that you are consistently encouraged; it is your inheritance in Christ. How can you enter, occupy, and be used in joy, courage, and confident faith? Develop a lifestyle that is joyfully resilient by receiving the steadfast love of the Lord.

🦁 Relax. Sit quietly, and allow the Holy Spirit to share his own desires and plans to encourage you.

Personal Notes

INNER ATMOSPHERE DETERMINES OUTER ENVIRONMENT

Manifesting our spirit to reveal what God has put inside of us is a deliberate act of faith. Warriors reveal their inner being in order to confront the enemy and help God do what He wants to do. Something exists inside each of us that must rise up in the face of trouble.

We see this same phenomenon centuries later when Jesus and His disciples crossed a lake in Mark 4:35–41:

> *That day when evening came, he said to his disciples, "Let us go over to the other side." Leaving the crowd behind, they took him along, just as he was, in the boat. There were also other boats with him.*
>
> *A furious squall came up, and the waves broke over the boat, so that it was nearly swamped. Jesus was in the stern, sleeping on a cushion. The disciples woke him and said to him, "Teacher, don't you care if we drown?"*
>
> *He got up, rebuked the wind and said to the waves, "Quiet! Be still!" Then the wind died down and it was completely calm.*

> *He said to his disciples, "Why are you so afraid? Do you still have no faith?" They were terrified and asked each other, "Who is this? Even the wind and the waves obey him!"*

The disciples, acting as another typology of our soulish nature, panicked in the storm and woke Jesus up. "Don't you care if we drown?" they asked, desperate to be delivered. Inside, the disciples blamed Jesus for not helping them. Similarly, the soul will blame everyone and everything for its troubles. Jesus, representing the spirit man, rebuked the winds and waves by sharing the peace He had on the inside. Out of that restful nature, He was able to bring rest to the situation around Him. He manifested what God had placed in His spirit.

We are not victims in our circumstances, but we can be victors. It is vital to position ourselves in the truth. We have Christ in us, not as a concept of truth, but as a reality of God's word. Christ in us releases a confident expectation that Heaven will come through for us as it did for Him.

We are learning to grow in that dynamic of trust and faith. We take care of the inner man and God takes care of his surroundings. We can start by positioning our will so that our mind is influenced by our spirit, and not by our circumstances. When we accomplish this, our mind uses our mouth to praise, confess, and declare God's greatness.

We each have a choice: will we magnify the Lord, or will we magnify the situation that is currently bothering us? Magnifying God is the antidote to a negative mindset. It turns a setback into a comeback. To live in the spirit, and to reveal our inner being, our whole person must be in agreement.

Faith is demonstrated by our entire person—soul, spirit, and body. With mental agreement and emotional submission, the action of our will agrees with the focus of the spirit and comes into alignment with who God is and what He wants to do. The instant this happens, breakthrough starts.

To magnify is part of our DNA. We will always magnify something, either positive or negative. We can turn a molehill into a mountain. We can make the opposition so big that we appear as grasshoppers in our own sight. Alternatively, we can see the Lord as He really is—high and lifted up, powerful, strong on our behalf—Almighty God.

Rejoicing always, giving thanks in all things, and being at rest and peace are all ways to develop an inner atmosphere of calm, joyful dependence upon the Lord. The important decision is to allow the Holy Spirit freedom to declare to you what the Father wants to be within the situation you are experiencing!

We all choose the experiences we want to have, whether through actual option or by default. If we allow experiences to be forced upon us by our failure to take control, then we have another set of problems to deal with as well as the original situation. An absence of internal focus leads us into a lifestyle of negative experiences that weigh heavily against our faith and confidence. We eventually come to a place where we cease to believe passionately and refrain from praying positively. We live in worldly hope—not true Christian hope, which is full of expectation.

We become unstable in all our ways. Life tosses us around from one fear to the next, like a piece of driftwood in the ocean. James 1:5–8:

> *But if any of you lacks wisdom, let him ask of God, who gives to all generously and without reproach, and it will be given to him.*

> *But he must ask in faith without any doubting, for the one who doubts is like the surf of the sea, driven and tossed by the wind.*

> *For that man ought not to expect that he will receive anything from the Lord, being a double-minded man, unstable in all his ways.*

We develop a single-minded focus on God's majesty as we worship who He essentially is in Himself. Then we move His majesty into our situation and begin to praise Him and declare His power. The inner atmosphere of our man of the spirit actively participates; and we generate faith, not only to ourselves and the situation, but to other people standing around watching.

When Jesus raised Lazarus from the dead, it was as much for the benefit of people present as for Lazarus himself! Jesus prayed in a particular way so that they could share in His partnership with the Father. Lazarus is diagnosed as terminally ill in verse two, and is raised from the dead in verse forty-four. In the intervening time frame Jesus is not responding to external requirements. He is listening to the Father only. He continues what He is doing and briefly sends a message "this sickness is not to end in death, but for the glory of God" [John 11:4].

Though He loved the family, He remained obedient to God. He made two other statements about Lazarus which revealed the depth of His inner calm in the spirit. John 11:11 and 14–15:

This He said, and after that He said to them, "Our friend Lazarus has fallen asleep; but I go, so that I may awaken him out of sleep."

So Jesus then said to them plainly, "Lazarus is dead, and I am glad for your sakes that I was not there, so that you may believe; but let us go to him."

He has a physical journey to make in order to return to Judea, but He has already made the journey in His inner man. "I go to awaken him." When we live in the intentionality of God, we are prepared for every circumstance, and the external pressure cannot affect us adversely. The fruit of self control prevents the enemy from making a nuisance of himself. It strips him of his power by simply focusing our intention on the Lord. Self control is pulling up the drawbridge to our interior castle, thus denying entry to any malicious or unbelieving voice.

"I am glad for your sakes…" Our inner man exists for the blessing and benefit of people around us. He knows that he will reap from what is sown and he has no intention of seeing that promise ruined by selfishness. God is no man's debtor. He loves to reward us. He loves to see us blessed and prospering. He teaches us a giving lifestyle so that He can reveal His abundance.

When the big moment came, Jesus drew everyone around Him into the action. He prayed in such an all inclusive way that people were drawn into the environment created by His inner man.

> *So they removed the stone. Then Jesus raised His eyes, and said, "Father, I thank You that You have heard Me.*
>
> *"I knew that You always hear Me; but because of the people standing around I said it, so that they may believe that You sent Me."*
>
> *When He had said these things, He cried out with a loud voice, "Lazarus, come forth."*

Remember, Jesus was not God pretending to be a man. He was actually a man in right relationship with God. As such, He was modeling in His own relationship with the Father, pre-cross, how we could expect to live in a post resurrection environment.

Our inner atmosphere determines our external environment. In this case, the inner presence of Jesus called all the shots for the external crowd around Him. They were drawn into the influence of His inner strength and faith. Something or Someone is going to dictate your circumstances. In Christ you are empowered to make right choices.

ASSIGNMENT

🦁 What experience do you wish to have in your current situation? What inner atmosphere do you need to develop in the course of your relationship with the Father? This is only hard work initially. Eventually (in a few weeks) it becomes normal and a part of your usual routine — like brushing your teeth and tying your shoelaces.

COMMISSION

🦁 Develop a routine of rejoicing throughout the day. Learn the simple art of giving thanks to the Lord in every circumstance. Make it your first response — thanking the Lord for who He is in Himself, for us, and in our circumstances. David used the Psalms that way. They are recorded responses to various circumstances. Make a list of responses that you can make internally to God specifically to challenge your present situation.

Personal Notes

FRUSTRATION

Frustration does not exist
    in the kingdom.
It is a device of the world,
    A negative construct contrary
to the nature of the Bright One.

Frustration is an admission that we
    are baffled, checked, blocked,
neutralized in faith—
    by people, circumstances, and opposition.
Frustration legitimizes negative emotions,
    giving them a place in our experience.

Frustration is discontent
    opening our heart to lethargy.
We become irked, resentful, disappointed,
    gullible to defeat—
Owned by pessimism.

We must learn how to use frustration
    and not be used by it.
To be frustrated is to admit
    that I do not possess at this moment
The required amount of patience, peace,
    and joy for the circumstances of my life.

If I focus on frustration,
    the core of my attention
Is the opposite of who God is for me.

Frustration is an emotional sign
    that I need an upgrade.
It points to an available increase,
    raising my awareness of God's provision.
Therefore, frustration must turn to
    celebration of God's intent.

In the hands of the enemy
    it robs me of enthusiasm.
It blinds me to all the possibilities
    of the one true Spirit.

I become disheartened, looking for
    pity, sympathy—
Seeking fellow victims of discouragement.
    I give permission to be afflicted.
Frustration causes negative fellowship
    as I move in the opposite spirit
To Christ within.

In the hands of the Shining One
    It points towards fullness,
The reality of something more —
    greater success unfolding.
Frustration is turned into confession
    in one stroke of happy thinking.

"Thank you, Father, that frustration
    reveals my lack of Your fullness.
It points me to the upgrade available.
    It releases Your permission to become more.

Patience, peace, and joy abound
    constantly in Your presence.
Grace follows the upgrade;
    love flows more powerfully.

I am renewed, restored, made bigger,
    enabled to see from a greater height
Of Your affection.
    Everything must bow
to patience, peace, and joy.
    They are Heaven's true reality."

Frustration is earthly, one dimensional,
    and destructive.
It reduces everything it touches.
    It makes us start everything
From a place of deficit.
    We struggle to catch up

With God's reality.
    Frustration is reality
From a wrong dimension.

To fight frustration we must turn
    our back on it,
Look into the heart of the One
    committed to our development,
Trade our sorrows for His joy.
    Frustration must turn to celebration.

Patience is the fast track to greater heights.
    Joy is the welcoming party to Presence.
Wisdom releases the focus of Heaven.
    Peace releases the angst,
Causing us to smile, be carefree.
    Contentment with godliness—
… a sure winner.

ASSIGNMENT

🛡 Check yourself out. Frustration makes people passive. Is there any area of your life that makes you feel powerless, neutralized in faith, and resentful?

🛡 Are you blaming others for your current circumstances? What is your negative confession regarding your relationship with Jesus and your own spirituality? How have you allowed yourself to be robbed of your enthusiasm and joy? Describe your emotional state at this time.

🛡 Frustration gives permission for the enemy to afflict us and our relationships. What negative fellowship have you allowed into your life with others?

COMMISSION

🛡 Use frustration; do not be used by it. If it is bound in Heaven, it can be bound on Earth. What can be loosed in Heaven over your present circumstances? [Matthew 16:19]

🛡 Look again at the prayer within the text. What is the upgrade that the Father wants to give you? How can you learn to use frustration and move in the opposite spirit?

🛡 What is the process by which the Holy Spirit will turn frustration into celebration? What is your part in this partnership?

🛡 Journal your responses and decisions.

PERSONAL NOTES

YOUR INTIMACY INTIMIDATES THE ENEMY

strong breakthrough spirit was on Caleb and Joshua in Numbers 13 and 14. Moses had sent twelve spies, including Caleb and Joshua, into the Promised Land. Ten of them returned with bad reports; they let their mind and emotions ratchet up fear among the people. In Numbers 13:27–29, they highlighted every difficulty the Israelites would face in conquering the land:

We went to the land where you sent us. It truly flows with milk and honey, and this is its fruit.

Nevertheless the people who dwell in the land are strong; the cities are fortified and very large; moreover we saw the descendants of Anak there.

The Amalekites dwell in the land of the South; the Hittites, the Jebusites, and the Amorites dwell in the mountains; and the Canaanites dwell by the sea and along the banks of the Jordan.

Caleb tried his best to stem the tide of terror that was building in the camp, but to no avail, as we read in verses 30–33:

> *Then Caleb quieted the people before Moses, and said, "Let us go up at once and take possession, for we are well able to overcome it."*
>
> *But the men who had gone up with him said, "We are not able to go up against the people, for they are stronger than we." And they gave the children of Israel a bad report of the land which they had spied out, saying, "The land through which we have gone as spies is a land that devours its inhabitants, and all the people whom we saw in it are men of great stature.*
>
> *There we saw the giants (the descendants of Anak came from the giants); and we were like grasshoppers in our own sight, and so we were in their sight."*

The next day, Joshua added his voice to Caleb's in one last attempt to convince his countrymen to step into the breakthrough God had promised them [Numbers 14:6–9]:

> *But Joshua the son of Nun and Caleb the son of Jephunneh, who were among those who had spied out the land, tore their clothes;*
>
> *and they spoke to all the congregation of the children of Israel, saying: "The land we passed through to spy out is an exceedingly good land.*
>
> *If the LORD delights in us, then He will bring us into this land and give it to us, 'a land which flows with milk and honey.'*

*Only do not rebel against the LORD, nor fear the people of
the land, for they are our bread; their protection has departed
from them, and the LORD is with us. Do not fear them."*

Nothing the enemy did had turned those spies into grasshoppers—instead, they had carried that mindset with them
into the Promised Land. Ten men managed to derail the plan
of God, turning their friends and neighbors into grumbling,
rebellious unbelievers. In their fear, they even contemplated
returning to Egypt; after all, it was better in their minds to
live in bondage than to die in battle.

Likewise, soulish Christians believe that it simply costs
too much to get free from the things that bind them. "Better to stay as I am," they think to themselves. They settle for
mediocrity in their relationship with God, their friendships,
their marriages, and their churches. They would rather sit
in bondage than pay the price to get free. They fail to realize that Jesus Himself has already paid for that freedom on
their behalf; they simply have to walk with Him through the
journey into that Promised Land.

Joshua and Caleb manifested what God had put in them:
courage and faith. They knew everything came down to one
simple issue— *"If the Lord delights in us…"* That was the
question they wrestled with. Is God pleased with us or not?
If He is, nothing can stop us.

I can answer that question for every believer. He is. God
is very pleased with each and every one of us. Why? Because
He only sees us in Jesus. He cannot see us separate from His
Son. Why wouldn't He be pleased with you?

Joshua knew this instinctively. He beseeched the other Israelites to stay the course. Instead, they rebelled against God and the leadership He had put in place. The Lord had no choice but to remove His hand of protection from them, leaving that rebellious generation to wander the desert for decades until every one of them had died—except for the faithful Joshua and Caleb.

Fear leads to rebellion. Faith, however, leads to occupation of the promises God has given us. Ten spies denied an entire nation access to the fulfillment of prophecy. Only two men from an entire generation inherited it. Those terrified, soulish spies prevented people from realizing their destiny. They stole the dreams of those people because they lived in their souls, not in their spirits.

Joshua and Caleb had one thing in common. They both practiced a level of intimacy with God. Caleb was a man of a different spirit because He loved the presence of God. Likewise Joshua would remain in the Tabernacle after Moses had left. Intimacy intimidates the enemy. Intimacy is the key to successful warfare. Both men cherished their relationship with God. They knew how to live in the place of delight and affirmation.

God loves to confirm His nature to us. Our intimacy with Him is built upon His intimacy with us. He loves to be close. He loves to declare who He is for us. His intention is always about a deeper relationship. He is totally committed to upgrading our experience of Him and to bringing us into a deeper place of rest, joy, and assurance in Him. He adores confident people and seeks to develop the capacity in us for trust and faith at a high level.

Intimacy is the key to warfare. It puts us into a place of faith before God as we lean into His majesty. All of Heaven is confident and full of rejoicing about the sovereignty of Almighty God. "On earth as it is in heaven" [Matthew 6:10] was the example of real praying that Jesus used to mentor His disciples.

Intimacy engages with God where He rules in Heaven. It is the joyful discipline of a resurrected lifestyle. We are focused on the life above, not the one beneath [Colossians 3:1–2]. Worship is focus—powerful focus. There is a discipline to worship, a retraining of our spirituality to empower us for a life of renewed focus. We are in the business of reinventing the way we live our lives before God. We are being renewed in the spirit of our mind.

All discipline has the potential to be enjoyed as we learn to focus on what we are gaining, not on what we are losing. Joshua and Caleb were looking forward to a fight that they knew they could not lose. They had such confidence in the personality of God! Intimacy breeds trust and confidence. This intimidates the enemy who hates worship, because when people fully engage in rejoicing, they become vulnerable to the Lord and immovable to the schemes of the enemy.

Worship fixes our heart. Intimacy inspires a steadfast spirit [Psalm 57:7]. We cannot lose when our focus is God. Rejoicing and giving of thanks inspires us to stand in the shadow of the Almighty.

ASSIGNMENT

🦁 What upgrade have you received in your relationship with the Lord? What upgrade is He planning for you? What are you facing in your current circumstances that would try to prevent you from inheriting from the Lord?

COMMISSION

🦁 It is vital to retrain yourself in rejoicing and giving of thanks. Where will you start? Pick a situation in your life. Lay it down before the Lord. Step away from it and turn your back on it.

🦁 Begin to worship God for who He is. Resist the urge to draw Him into your circumstances. Instead let Him draw you into a place of majesty.

🦁 Record what changes this makes in your spirit.

PERSONAL NOTES

Personal Notes

A WARRIOR'S PERCEPTION OF REALITY

Spiritual warriors do not get distracted; they are focused on waiting on God. Their eyes are searching for Him in every situation. Where is God? What does He want to do? They allow themselves to be drawn by the Spirit. Because these warriors know how to find God in even the most difficult situations, they can break through for themselves—and for other people.

Our ability to line up with God's will is what causes us to break through. There are no easy wins in life. If a Christian has a lazy, flabby will that needs building up, they will have to exercise it through some hard times. The more we exercise our will, the stronger our focus on God becomes.

Faith and focus depend on will and spirit combining. The enemy will always attack our mind and emotions in order to subvert the will. He knows that if he loses his grip on a human's will, he will be in trouble. But to outright attack someone's will is difficult; manipulating it through emotions and mindset is much easier.

Spiritual warriors, when under extreme pressure, rely on God's will to work on their own. They know that victory only comes from a will that submits to the Spirit of God. No one can manifest anything in their spirit if their own will is working against them.

David's psalms are an example of a man talking to himself, convincing himself of God's greatness. They show us how to reach out in strength, even when we ourselves are mired in weakness. When a Christian is feeling out of sorts, we ought to be radical enough to find someone with a similar problem and pray for them. When we declare God's truth to someone else, that truth will rebound back to us. I never understood why Christians stay home from meetings when they are sick. Why not go and pray for someone who is even more ill than you? You have a better chance of being healed if you yourself are praying for someone else to be healed.

The act of reaching out in praise or ministry makes us susceptible to the Holy Spirit. None of us can whine and win; we have to make a choice. Too many Christians allow what they cannot do to get in the way of what they can do.

Great warriors, on the other hand, focus on the process, not the end result. They know that life in the spirit is all about taking the next step, however small it may seem at the time. God does not stipulate what size the step is going to be, He just encourages us to keep on walking toward Him. While most believers just want the process of life to be over so they can reap the reward, spiritual warriors enjoy the journey every bit as much as the victory.

God is not interested in simply helping people to a destination. He is acutely concerned with how we get there and wants to be with us on that journey. In Luke 24, Jesus wasn't walking with His disciples in order to get to Emmaus; He was walking with them because He enjoyed their company and wanted to share the Good News of His resurrection. When we ask God to do something quickly, He usually says "No." Most of us want our problems resolved overnight so that life can go back to normal. God simply does not work that way. He wants to walk the trail with us, giving us wisdom, revelation, and His presence.

We are not designed to have merely functional relationships in the kingdom. God is highly relational, and so intimacy must be the highest priority of life in the spirit. We have two relationships with God. One is vertical, one-on-one with God Himself. The other is horizontal, through loving and interacting with others. If we say we love God, we ought also to love one another [1 John 4:11]. When we love one another we are proving our love for God.

To live with God is to share His reality. We must seek the Lord for His perception of what we are going through. We live by words. They can be negative and defeating. Numbers 13:31–33:

> *But the men who had gone up with him said, "We are not able to go up against the people, for they are too strong for us."*
>
> *So they gave out to the sons of Israel a bad report of the land which they had spied out, saying, "The land through which we have gone, in spying it out, is a land that devours its*

> *inhabitants; and all the people whom we saw in it are men*
> *of great size.*
>
> *"There also we saw the Nephilim (the sons of Anak are part*
> *of the Nephilim); and we became like grasshoppers in our*
> *own sight, and so we were in their sight."*

When we lose our perspective we do more than lose a battle. We lose our identity and our inheritance. We become weak and powerless, willing to make ourselves vulnerable to a tyrant, rather than face up to what is preventing us from receiving abundance. "Better to return to Egypt" is the cry of a person who has lost perspective.

We live by every word that proceeds from the mouth of God [Matthew 4:4]. Jesus only spoke what the Father said. It is the power of agreement. Words can be uplifting and fill us with courage. Warriors who see how God sees, that is who perceive in the spirit, are able to release others to see the same thing and be changed by it.

2 Kings 6:15–17 is the story of two men in a very dangerous situation. One is able to perceive in the spirit a reality that God is enjoying, the other man is without perception.

> *Now when the attendant of the man of God had risen early*
> *and gone out, behold, an army with horses and chariots was*
> *circling the city. And his servant said to him, "Alas, my*
> *master! What shall we do?"*
>
> *So he answered, "Do not fear, for those who are with us are*
> *more than those who are with them."*
>
> *Then Elisha prayed and said, "O Lord, I pray, open his eyes*
> *that he may see." And the Lord opened the servant's eyes*

and he saw; and behold, the mountain was full of horses and chariots of fire all around Elisha.

ASSIGNMENT

🦁 Read the above passage and think deeply on it. What do you think happened within the servant when he could perceive properly? How do you think it would change him? If you were that servant what difference would it make to your life to have a warrior's perspective?

COMMISSION

🦁 What is your level of perception about your own situation at this time? What more do you need to see about God and yourself? How is the Father using these circumstances to upgrade your identity? What part of your inheritance is currently at stake, awaiting fresh perspective?

🦁 Journal your way into an upgraded identity:

PERSONAL NOTES

WARRIORS PROVE GOD'S DOMINANCE

T*he Old Testament is full* of examples of the Spirit of God coming upon an individual for the purpose of breakthrough and deliverance. In 2 Chronicles 20, for example, Judah was under siege by three powerful nations. The Hebrews were so terrified that they gathered to beg God for help, their children clinging to them in fear. After calling out to God, He answered, as we read in verses 14–19:

> *Then the Spirit of the LORD came upon Jahaziel the son of Zechariah, the son of Benaiah, the son of Jeiel, the son of Mattaniah, a Levite of the sons of Asaph, in the midst of the assembly.*
>
> *And he said, "Listen, all you of Judah and you inhabitants of Jerusalem, and you, King Jehoshaphat! Thus says the LORD to you: 'Do not be afraid nor dismayed because of this great multitude, for the battle is not yours, but God's.*

> *Tomorrow go down against them. They will surely come up by the Ascent of Ziz, and you will find them at the end of the brook before the Wilderness of Jeruel.*
>
> *You will not need to fight in this battle. Position yourselves, stand still and see the salvation of the LORD, who is with you, O Judah and Jerusalem!' Do not fear or be dismayed; tomorrow go out against them, for the LORD is with you."*
>
> *And Jehoshaphat bowed his head with his face to the ground, and all Judah and the inhabitants of Jerusalem bowed before the LORD, worshiping the LORD.*
>
> *Then the Levites of the children of the Kohathites and of the children of the Korahites stood up to praise the LORD God of Israel with voices loud and high.*

The battle went exactly as Jahaziel prophesied. Because he manifested his spirit and sought God for breakthrough, deliverance happened. In a heartbeat, the nation turned from mourning and trembling to proclamation and praise.

A spiritual warrior shows others the gap between what is real and what is perception. In 1 Kings 18, Elijah went to the top of Mount Carmel to prove his God's dominance over Baal. Outnumbered 450 to 1, Elijah never blinked in the face of opposition. He started by challenging his people in verse 21:

> *"And Elijah came to all the people, and said, 'How long will you falter between two opinions? If the LORD is God, follow Him; but if Baal, follow him.' But the people answered him not a word."*

Unhappy with that answer, Elijah set out to prove God's sovereignty, as we read in verses 22–39:

Then Elijah said to the people, "I alone am left a prophet of
the LORD; but Baal's prophets are four hundred and fifty
men.

Therefore let them give us two bulls; and let them choose one
bull for themselves, cut it in pieces, and lay it on the wood,
but put no fire under it; and I will prepare the other bull,
and lay it on the wood, but put no fire under it.

Then you call on the name of your gods, and I will call on
the name of the LORD; and the God who answers by fire,
He is God."

So all the people answered and said, "It is well spoken."

Now Elijah said to the prophets of Baal, "Choose one bull for
yourselves and prepare it first, for you are many; and call on
the name of your god, but put no fire under it."

So they took the bull which was given them, and they prepared
it, and called on the name of Baal from morning even till
noon, saying, "O Baal, hear us!" But there was no voice; no
one answered. Then they leaped about the altar which they
had made.

And so it was, at noon, that Elijah mocked them and said,
"Cry aloud, for he is a god; either he is meditating, or he is
busy, or he is on a journey, or perhaps he is sleeping and must
be awakened."

So they cried aloud, and cut themselves, as was their custom,
with knives and lances, until the blood gushed out on them.

And when midday was past, they prophesied until the time of
the offering of the evening sacrifice. But there was no voice;
no one answered, no one paid attention.

87

Then Elijah said to all the people, "Come near to me." So all the people came near to him. And he repaired the altar of the LORD that was broken down.

And Elijah took twelve stones, according to the number of the tribes of the sons of Jacob, to whom the word of the LORD had come, saying, "Israel shall be your name."

Then with the stones he built an altar in the name of the LORD; and he made a trench around the altar large enough to hold two seahs of seed.

And he put the wood in order, cut the bull in pieces, and laid it on the wood, and said, "Fill four waterpots with water, and pour it on the burnt sacrifice and on the wood."

Then he said, "Do it a second time," and they did it a second time; and he said, "Do it a third time," and they did it a third time.

So the water ran all around the altar; and he also filled the trench with water.

And it came to pass, at the time of the offering of the evening sacrifice, that Elijah the prophet came near and said, "LORD God of Abraham, Isaac, and Israel, let it be known this day that You are God in Israel and I am Your servant, and that I have done all these things at Your word:

Hear me, O LORD, hear me, that this people may know that You are the LORD God, and that You have turned their hearts back to You again."

Then the fire of the LORD fell and consumed the burnt sacrifice, and the wood and the stones and the dust, and it licked up the water that was in the trench.

Now when all the people saw it, they fell on their faces; and they said, "The LORD, He is God! The LORD, He is God!"

Elijah's boldness transformed his countrymen's perception of God. He set up the test and manifested what God had given him—courage in the face of adversity. He was so confident in God's plan that he let the false prophets go first. As they struggled and saw no results, he mocked them.

When it was Elijah's turn, he made things even tougher for himself. He had water poured all over his altar and sacrifice. Still, the instant he called on God's fire, it came. Israel's people, stunned by the faith Elijah had shown, immediately repented. He broke the power of the occult in that moment.

Do not try to make things easier for God, trust in His majesty. Stand in His sovereignty. We step into situations under the unction of the Holy Spirit. We are not there to make things happen. We are present in order to trust God. When we manifest our spirit, it is always towards the Father. We are in Christ, partnering with the Father, through the Holy Spirit. We reveal that identity in the circumstances.

We demonstrate confidence which leads to particular boldness. At other times in our weakness we step into a place of God's strength by simply trusting Him. He will never leave us nor forsake us. He is with us always—especially when we cannot feel His presence. We get to take His word on trust, which is a really safe place from which to live and act!

Firstly, we face God and revel in who He is in Himself. Then we proclaim who He is for us. We rejoice in His heart toward us. We give thanks in His Name and Nature to us.

Then we declare who He is within us. We step into our identity as much loved children, sons, and heirs of God in Christ.

Then we face the issue. We are taller; it has reduced in size. Our perspective in God opens up a greater reality, and we step into the place of revelation and power in partnership with Him. Warriors prove God's majesty. We don't just point to it. We step into it and are embraced by God's strength. When David strengthened himself in the Lord, that was the process he went through to receive an upgrade from a higher dimension [1 Samuel 30:6–8]. When his perspective had changed, he was able to receive prophetic instruction about how to act in his circumstances.

Our weakness is not an obstacle to God. Our lack of trust gives Him nothing to work with in our circumstances. It is important to stand with God. There will be times when we stand in confidence and times when we connect in our weakness. Trust is always the issue. We start with who God is in Himself, and the Holy Spirit moves us into the process that leads us to manifest who God is within our inner man.

ASSIGNMENT

🦁 What would be the dominant thought/belief about the Father that would overshadow your circumstances? What would it mean for you to live in the shadow of that revelation?

COMMISSION

🦁 To prove God's dominance, your identity needs an upgrade. How will you strengthen yourself in the Lord at this time? What aspect of God's dominance will be revealed to you and through you?

🦁 Follow the process of renewal outlined in this chapter and journal its effect on you in your circumstances.

PERSONAL NOTES

PERSONAL NOTES

WE SHOULD NOT BE DEFLECTED FROM PURPOSE

*A*lways take your cue from God. In difficult circumstances most of the advice given can be about rescue; about being safe; about being careful. When we live in the right place in the Father's heart we are more concerned with learning to be carefree than careful. People unconsciously put upon us their own fears and worries. Though well meant, it is still oppositional in nature. It is acting against God's purposes.

In Acts 21:1–14, Paul pushed back against some of that same fearful opposition:

> *Now it came to pass, that when we had departed from them and set sail, running a straight course we came to Cos, the following day to Rhodes, and from there to Patara.*
>
> *And finding a ship sailing over to Phoenicia, we went aboard and set sail.*
>
> *When we had sighted Cyprus, we passed it on the left, sailed to Syria, and landed at Tyre; for there the ship was to unload her cargo.*

> *And finding disciples, we stayed there seven days. They told Paul through the Spirit not to go up to Jerusalem.*
>
> *When we had come to the end of those days, we departed and went on our way; and they all accompanied us, with wives and children, till we were out of the city. And we knelt down on the shore and prayed.*
>
> *When we had taken our leave of one another, we boarded the ship, and they returned home.*
>
> *And when we had finished our voyage from Tyre, we came to Ptolemais, greeted the brethren, and stayed with them one day.*
>
> *On the next day we who were Paul's companions departed and came to Caesarea, and entered the house of Philip the evangelist, who was one of the seven, and stayed with him.*
>
> *Now this man had four virgin daughters who prophesied.*
>
> *And as we stayed many days, a certain prophet named Agabus came down from Judea.*
>
> *When he had come to us, he took Paul's belt, bound his own hands and feet, and said, "Thus says the Holy Spirit, 'So shall the Jews at Jerusalem bind the man who owns this belt, and deliver him into the hands of the Gentiles.'"*
>
> *Now when we heard these things, both we and those from that place pleaded with him not to go up to Jerusalem.*
>
> *Then Paul answered, "What do you mean by weeping and breaking my heart? For I am ready not only to be bound, but also to die at Jerusalem for the name of the Lord Jesus."*
>
> *So when he would not be persuaded, we ceased, saying, "The will of the Lord be done."*

The disciples who argued with Paul spoke only out of their soul. They were emotional at the thought of losing their dear friend, but Paul had a clear vision of what God wanted to do with his life. He was ready to give everything to the Christ he had encountered on the road to Damascus.

Spiritual warriors cannot be deflected from their God-given purpose. Even death itself was irrelevant to Paul, for he had a clear vision of who God wanted to be inside of him.

Inside every believer is something that needs to rise up. We are not paupers; we are the people of God. We are not poor; we are His Beloved children. If we practice living out of our spirit, we will become a move of God.

We are led by the Spirit ultimately. We may seek advice obviously, but we must do so carefully. There is no substitute for our own relational searching of God's heart for us. Other people act as a confirmation of God's intent, but we need to discover His objective for ourselves.

In relationship His will is made known to us. In friendship with people it is confirmed. When the Lord is requiring something difficult of us we must be especially careful of the advice we take. The Father has three options regarding our progress in a situation. They are: yes, no, and wait. None of them are cautionary.

In full permission we press on towards the high calling. When God says "No," to us, it may be for several reasons. It may be that He has something bigger for us to see. It may be that we need to grow up more in Christ. "Wait," is usually a timing issue as well as preparatory.

We are following the will of God, not the fears and caution of man. There will be times when the will of God for us will conflict with the blessings, freedoms, and permissions of people around us. If we pursue God's will against advice, we can be labeled as rebellious—even arrogant.

It is hard to conform to something that is rooted in a negative. In my own circumstances, problems have arisen because people failed to see my emerging identity and destiny. It is hard to be in a community that does not own your progress. It is tough to stay around people who have stopped moving themselves, when your own identity is calling you to go further up and further in.

Church history is full of stories of people who went against established advice and found the fullness of God.

ASSIGNMENT

🦁 What is the direction in which you are headed? What are the pitfalls of attempting the journey? What is the outcome that the Father has promised you? What are the promises and permissions that have been placed on this journey ahead of you?

COMMISSION

🦁 What is God's purpose for you at this time? Are you waiting for God, or is He waiting on you? Come to a place of rest and stillness. Pray, and ask for reassurance. Let peace be the umpire; follow its decision.

🦁 Journal what the Lord is saying to you.

PERSONAL NOTES

PERSONAL NOTES

WEAKNESS CANNOT PREVENT US FROM OVERCOMING

W*e are never asked to* live from a negative. We are always hugely encouraged to trust, be in faith, and believe. God believes the best about us even though we are constantly in transition. We are in Christ, learning to be Christ-like. We are being changed from one degree of glory to another. We are totally loved in that process, even if we are struggling to become more of who we are in Christ.

We are not asked to live from a place of weakness. We are encouraged to discover God's strength to us. The grace of God is so compellingly powerful towards us; it actually overrules every negative perspective.

The world is focused on weakness as the key place to begin the process of change. The kingdom focuses on strength as the major key to transformation. That power is perfected in weakness means that strength flows into what we are not. The result of God's life erupting within is that we boast about our weakness in the context of the amazing power of Christ within [2 Corinthians 12:9–10].

We take pleasure in our weaknesses; we are not downhearted about them. The reason is—the Father. His love is so incredible, so astonishing, it reaches out to us in our sinfulness and pulls us into His embrace. From that place we discover that we are the Beloved of God. It is our privilege to go through life, fully loved. This is fabulous news. All our change procedures come through being loved incredibly.

It is important to love change and the process of learning. If we do all our changes in the love of God we are always excited about who God is for us and who we are becoming in Him. He chose us in our weakness and loves to meet those needs with His strength. He strengthens us with His presence in our low places. He does not give us strength; He becomes our strength.

My weakness is the low place where God steps into my inadequacy. He inhabits that place with His own courage, firmness, and power. If He were to leave that space in my life, I would still be weak. The increase, the upgrade, that I receive in that area is not because He has given me something to fill that gap in my life. He is my increase in Himself.

Relationally, He inhabits my weaknesses, and I learn the pleasure of His presence. I can boast about my shortcomings because in Christ I am learning how to turn an inadequacy into a joyful vulnerability. For example, I do not possess an ability to think quickly on my feet. I have to study a question for quite a while before I understand it. This is a legacy of a hammer attack when I was a much younger man. I was hit so hard that a part of my brain simply does not function properly, including my short term memory.

I am constantly being put into situations where people need counsel, advice, and general wisdom. Many times I do not understand the question. However, the grace upon my life has empowered me to experience the Father in a significant way in this area. I do not listen to the question; I listen to the Lord. I hear the question, but I do not have to process it. I open my heart to the Lord, and I say what He says. On occasions now too numerous to count, I have given a really helpful word of wisdom without even understanding the question. Take away that grace and presence, and I am still the same old Graham who doesn't have a clue what is happening. That's funny! And it's wonderful! In my weakness I can boast in who God is for me, to me, and in me.

It is a wonderful culture of dependency to which the Father wishes to commit us, that empowers us to be as brilliant in Him in all of our low places. What a great life He has given us! His presence is our increase. We get to abide in Him. He fills a space that I cannot fill. Everything that is meant to rob or disempower me instead becomes my place of praise, rejoicing, and laughter. Insults can be fun. Distress is downgraded by rest and peace. In persecutions we get to overcome and take ground. In difficulties we learn faithfulness, patience, and stamina which are all the qualities we need to become more than conquerors.

Our dependency upon Him must be total. When we are weak, we are also at a higher point of strength—in Him.

Christ in us gives us an expectation of something brilliant occurring.

God calls me in my weakness, then calls Himself to meet my needs in those places. My weakness is His calling on my life. Weakness and strength form an amazing paradox that we are to enjoy, not endure. A paradox is two seemingly opposing ideas contained in the same truth. We have to die to live, give to receive, be last in order to be first. The church is both a building and a body. The first is rigid, inflexible, and unmovable. The second is fluid, flexible, and constantly changing. We need both sides of a paradox at work in us. It is not a question of either/or, but of both/and. The issue in a paradox is what takes precedence at any one time, and that is determined by the presence of God—not circumstances. In the paradox of Mary and Martha, Jesus made His will clear. "You will not always have me like this, so you need to choose me now!" The one thing that is necessary is always chosen by God. We are learning therefore to listen and obey.

Paul's personal weakness paradox can be seen in his overlying attitude toward himself and God. On one hand he can state, "I was with you in weakness and in fear and in much trembling," [1 Corinthians 2:3]. And he can also write, "I can do all things in Christ through Him who strengthens me," [Philippians 4:13]. Ephesians 3:8–10 states:

> *To me, the very least of all saints, this grace was given, to preach to the Gentiles the unfathomable riches of Christ, and to bring to light what is the administration of the mystery which for ages has been hidden in God who created all things; so that the manifold wisdom of God might now be made*

known through the church to the rulers and the authorities
in the heavenly places.

This is a wonderful paradox. "I am the very least of all saints," [Ephesians 3:8] and yet, "I consider myself not in the least inferior to the most eminent apostles," [2 Corinthians 11:5]. He never forgot that he persecuted the church and held the coats of those who stoned Stephen. Yet he had the greatest understanding of grace and weakness. His ability to rest in Christ's strength was what opened him up to receive mysteries and learn things that were hidden. He was never stressed in his weakness because His focus was on enjoying who God was for him. We make a difference through our rest and peace in who Jesus is for us in the course of life.

We are to be "strengthened with power in the inner man through His Spirit" so that we can comprehend and know the amazing fullness of the love of God [Ephesians 3:16–20]. The Father seeks to commit us to an experience of His glory. In every encounter He becomes a revelation to our inner nature. He exposes us to His goodness, power, and wisdom. We are to become familiar with how His mind and heart function with us relationally. His goal is our direct participation with the fullness of Heaven. We are to be a people who live above circumstances. We are not earthbound but have a perspective from Heaven that overwhelms and overcomes everything against us, including our own insecurity and inadequacy.

He commits us to a journey of exploration and discovery into the passion of His love for us. It covers every square inch in every direction of our lives. It overwhelms all that we know, perceive, and understand so that we are immersed in the power and beauty of His compelling love. He fills all things with Himself. Abundance is a requirement. He wants a people who can live with the pressure of fullness—whom He can trust with everything.

Enjoying your weakness in the context of His abundance provides a necessary humility that sustains us under attack. We are exalted in our humility and are lifted up above the heads of our enemy. Our weakness is where we encounter abundance. Our worship increases when we are partakers of His presence in our low places. He steps into all that we are not with all that He is, and we are saved.

ASSIGNMENT

🦁 What are the low places of your life where you have not experienced the breakthrough of His presence for you? What would it look like for the Lord to fill you with Himself? What would it look like for you to be "strengthened with power through His Spirit in the inner man?"

COMMISSION

🦁 How can your weaknesses be perfected (matured) by God's power? What is the place of dependence and reliance to which you must come in order to enjoy this lifestyle?

🦁 What must you undo in your thinking and behavior regarding independence and self help in order to humbly and joyfully turn your inadequacy into a joyful vulnerability?

🦁 We can only enjoy our weaknesses if God enjoys our weaknesses. What does that mean to you?

🦁 Think hard and happily, and expand your thoughts *(journal your answers)*:

Personal Notes

THE ART OF THINKING POWERFULLY

In Romans 12:1–2, Paul laid out the importance of leading with our spirit, not our soul:

I beseech you therefore, brethren, by the mercies of God, that you present your bodies a living sacrifice, holy, acceptable to God, which is your reasonable service.

And do not be conformed to this world, but be transformed by the renewing of your mind, that you may prove what is that good and acceptable and perfect will of God.

When our soul submits to our spirit, we think differently. In essence, we are transformed by this renewing of our mind.

Blessings can and do occur in the most difficult circumstances, but we need a renewed mind to see and accept these gifts. Otherwise, we end up only focused on the immediate discomfort that is present. A spiritual warrior stands still long enough to focus his attention on God and find out what He is doing in the situation.

Manifesting our spirit releases wisdom and enables us to see and respond to what God is doing. It gives us a clearer perspective of God's desire. When we resist God, a contraction occurs; we get smaller in the spirit. But when we submit to the spirit, an expansion happens. Our heart is enlarged as we submit to God's hand. Our faith increases. We grow so rapidly that we push the enemy's territory into itself. The space in which he works contracts. Suddenly, the enemy has no room to operate. "The prince of this world is coming. He has no hold on me, but the world must learn that I love the Father and that I do exactly what my Father has commanded me," Jesus said in John 14:30–31.

Likewise, the enemy has no hold on a spiritual warrior who is doing what his Father has commanded. When we submit to God's hand, we can see clearly into His heart for us. Life in Christ is not about primarily discovering what God is doing, but rather about exploring who He is and specifically, who He wants to be for us now!

He manifests His spirit to us. Literally, He reveals Himself to our heart, and we are touched by His desire for us. Like a flower opening up to the sun, we are unlocked by the beauty of His love for us. To renew our mind we must be engaged with the mind of Christ. We are renewed in the spirit of our thinking when God is the object of our mindset.

Living out of our soul is a lower order of engagement because we are the primary focus. Our preoccupation with what we lack actually drives us away from God's desire for us. We feel unworthy, dissatisfied, discouraged, mentally and emotionally tired.

When we reckon ourselves dead to our old nature and alive to God [Romans 6:11] we become aware of all the possibilities that exist for us in the smile of God. Being aware of God's heart is refreshing, empowering, and cheerful. We feel His joy as a tangible expression of His goodness to us. He loves because He is love. His eternal joyfulness radiates peace and acceptance. We learn to live under His constant smile, and His affection makes us laugh on the journey of becoming more.

We become what we behold about God and ourselves. This is true, of course, whether positive or negative. To be renewed in the spirit of our mind is to always engage with the positive. God has not asked us to deal with the negative aspects of our lives. He has already dealt with them in Christ. We are dead to sin. He has crucified us with Christ. Our old nature is dead and buried. It is no longer our concern. We are in Christ learning to become Christ-like. Our whole engagement of life is to be created in the image of God. It is the ultimate reinvention.

Every day our primary focus is on living under God's smile and engaging with the Christ-life within. It is a process of discovery. We are exploring Jesus and who He is for us. When the Holy Spirit points to a part of our life that is not working, He is not pointing out our sin. He is not exposing us; He is manifesting the Father. He is exposing the warmth, the beauty, and the radiance of who God is for us. He is also pointing out the site of our next miracle of grace. He is indicating our next transformation.

Conversion of our thinking, to God's thinking, is the crucial element in all transformations. The Father has dealt with sin once and for all in Christ. Now He is dealing with life in all its beauty, grace, and power.

We are learning the art of thinking powerfully. We are becoming engaged more fully with the mind of Christ. Jesus exposed Himself to the wonder and majesty of the Father. He lives in that place of radiant light. Whatever He heard, He spoke. Whatever He saw, He did. It was His sustenance—more important than meat or drink.

Before we can manifest our spirit in the circumstances of life, we must become fully exposed to God's light within and over our own minds and hearts. We are not asked to engage with a negative. We are requested to become fully absorbed with the life of Christ.

Colossians 3:1–4:

Therefore if you have been raised up with Christ, keep seeking the things above, where Christ is seated at the right hand of God.

Set your mind on the things above, not on the things that are on earth. For you have died and your life is hidden with Christ in God.

When Christ, who is our life, is revealed, then you also will be revealed with Him in glory.

Colossians 2:9–15:

For in Him all the fullness of Deity dwells in bodily form, and in Him you have been made complete, and He is the head over all rule and authority; and in Him you were also circumcised with a circumcision made without hands, in the removal of the body of the flesh by the circumcision of Christ;

having been buried with Him in baptism, in which you were also raised up with Him through faith in the working of God, who raised Him from the dead.

When you were dead in your transgressions and the uncircumcision of your flesh, He made you alive together with Him, having forgiven us all our transgressions,

having canceled out the certificate of debt consisting of decrees against us, which was hostile to us; and He has taken it out of the way, having nailed it to the cross.

When He had disarmed the rulers and authorities, He made a public display of them, having triumphed over them through Him.

Romans 6:5–11:

For if we have become united with Him in the likeness of His death, certainly we shall also be in the likeness of His resurrection,

knowing this, that our old self was crucified with Him, in order that our body of sin might be done away with,

so that we would no longer be slaves to sin; for he who has died is freed from sin.

Now if we have died with Christ, we believe that we shall also live with Him,

knowing that Christ, having been raised from the dead, is never to die again; death no longer is master over Him.

For the death that He died, He died to sin once for all; but the life that He lives, He lives to God. Even so consider yourselves to be dead to sin, but alive to God in Christ Jesus.

2 Corinthians 5:14–21:

For the love of Christ controls us, having concluded this, that one died for all, therefore all died;

and He died for all, so that they who live might no longer live for themselves, but for Him who died and rose again on their behalf.

Therefore from now on we recognize no one according to the flesh; even though we have known Christ according to the flesh, yet now we know Him in this way no longer.

Therefore if anyone is in Christ, he is a new creature; the old things passed away; behold, new things have come.

Now all these things are from God, who reconciled us to Himself through Christ and gave us the ministry of reconciliation, namely, that God was in Christ reconciling the world to Himself, not counting their trespasses against them, and He has committed to us the word of reconciliation.

Therefore, we are ambassadors for Christ, as though God were making an appeal through us; we beg you on behalf of Christ, be reconciled to God.

He made Him who knew no sin to be sin on our behalf, so that we might become the righteousness of God in Him.

Our goal is to become the righteousness of God in Christ. We are focused on holiness, not sin. We are engrossed with the new nature of Christ, not the old nature that is dead. So, if a man has a problem with lust, he does not deal with it as a negative. He does not engage with it, receive counsel for it, learn to overcome it. He has lust because He is missing something about himself. He has not understood nor experienced his purity in Jesus. He has not fully engaged with righteousness.

He does not deal with lust; he engages with purity. He renounces the old behavior and submits to the power of the new nature with the amazing help of the Holy Spirit. We confess the old nature is dead. In prayer we are cut off from old behavior, and we begin to soak in the holiness of God. As we engage with a new mindset, our behavior becomes fully new and we develop the joyful habit of purity. Our mindset becomes new. Actions follow thoughts. New mindset, new behavior—the essence of transformation.

All the time we are engaging with what we are not, our mind has no possibility for transformation.

The art of powerful thinking lavishes itself on the personality and provision of Jesus. As He is, so are we. We become fully absorbed in the Name and Nature of Christ. We enjoy the journey. We are fully engrossed in who He is for us. We are grateful when the Holy Spirit points to a part of our life that is not working. Hope rises within us. It's time for change, and all transformations start with a superb thought about God and who He is for us.

It's exciting, energizing, and compelling in its beauty. It is the loving restoration to a higher glory. It is important to be thrilled about change, to love the learning. Process is a happy event! We are putting on Christ and experiencing Heaven on Earth as part of the process. Joy is at the heart of all our God encounters. Love is the result of His smile upon us. We are free to change, free to think incredible thoughts about ourselves in the fullness of who God is for us.

In the place of His deep affection, we cannot feel unworthy. We are accepted in the Beloved [Ephesians 1:6]. Being loved of God is therefore our starting point for transformation. There is no performance here, no earning of love or grace. It is the place where we stand and relax in His goodness.

We learn to be, before we start to do. It is vital that the Father washes over us. The right word will cleanse us. The wrong one makes us feel soiled. That's how we know when the Lord is speaking through someone. If there is no encounter with goodness, then it is not God; and we must continue listening. It is the goodness and the kindness of God that leads us to repentance.

Repentance is thinking again, having a better thought. It is a key part to transformation—renewing our thinking. All thinking must be rooted in God's goodness and kindness. Change is so much more enjoyable when we begin with the desired outcome and work back to our present condition. A pathway opens up in the loving-kindness of God. The future is never in doubt when we observe it through the lens of God's perspective in Christ. We think of it in the same way that He does. We run towards it as David ran towards Goliath. He did not see a giant; he saw the majesty of God and ran to meet it.

He engaged with God, not Goliath. There was no possibility of defeat. Goliath would go the same way as the lion and the bear. The enemy is defenseless against the majesty of God. When we become vulnerable to the same glory, we are strengthened through the intimacy of our encounter. Our intimacy, in turn, intimidates the enemy.

When God is the object of our thinking, the power that flows from a renewed mindset increases our relationship with Him; and we are radically changed.

ASSIGNMENT

🦁 Choose an area of your thinking that needs an upgrade and ask the Father to renew your mind in that place. What is the best thought you can have?

COMMISSION

🦁 How will the above thought(s) change your behavior? How will they affect the way you stand before God and position yourself in your circumstances?

Personal Notes

MEEKNESS: YOUR SECRET WEAPON

While the word *"warrior" conjures* up images of strength and power, meekness is actually the secret weapon of a spiritual warrior. When we learn how to be a lamb before God, we grow in spiritual authority. "Go your way; behold, I send you out as lambs among wolves," Jesus told His disciples in Luke 10:3. Most of us think that to be mighty in God, we have to be some sort of powerful superhero, but that is simply untrue. A lamb is a defenseless little thing that relies on its shepherd to keep it safe. What better metaphor could exist for a follower of Christ?

Jesus furthered that metaphor in Matthew 10:16: "Behold, I send you out as sheep in the midst of wolves. Therefore be wise as serpents and harmless as doves." God wants us to face our enemy, not with aggression, but with love and gentleness. We can survive as a lamb among wolves because our best friend is a lion. No wolf will attack us when we live under the shadow of a lion that promised He would never leave nor forsake us.

God will protect and keep us. We need only remember the words of Psalm 91 to know that truth:

He who dwells in the secret place of the Most High shall abide under the shadow of the Almighty.

I will say of the LORD, "He is my refuge and my fortress; my God, in Him I will trust."

Surely He shall deliver you from the snare of the fowler and from the perilous pestilence.

He shall cover you with His feathers, and under His wings you shall take refuge; His truth shall be your shield and buckler.

You shall not be afraid of the terror by night, nor of the arrow that flies by day, nor of the pestilence that walks in darkness, nor of the destruction that lays waste at noonday.

A thousand may fall at your side, and ten thousand at your right hand; but it shall not come near you.

Only with your eyes shall you look, and see the reward of the wicked.

Because you have made the LORD, who is my refuge, even the Most High, your dwelling place,

No evil shall befall you, nor shall any plague come near your dwelling; for He shall give His angels charge over you, to keep you in all your ways.

In their hands they shall bear you up, lest you dash your foot against a stone.

You shall tread upon the lion and the cobra, the young lion and the serpent you shall trample underfoot.

Because he has set his love upon Me, therefore I will deliver him; I will set him on high, because he has known My name.

He shall call upon Me, and I will answer him; I will be with him in trouble; I will deliver him and honor him.

With long life I will satisfy him, and show him My salvation.

God will protect and keep us. A lamb offers an intriguing picture of our response to God. Lambs are meek, humble, and gentle. They are growing and curious. These same qualities occur when a man or woman is broken before God. Meekness is not weakness—it is strength under control. Moses was the meekest man on the face of the Earth, and yet he led millions of people. "Now the man Moses was very humble, more than all men who were on the face of the earth," records Numbers 12:3.

"Blessed are the meek, for they shall inherit the earth," Jesus said in Matthew 5:5. "Take My yoke upon you and learn from Me, for I am gentle and lowly in heart, and you will find rest for your souls," He added in Matthew 11:29.

Meekness occurs when we put God first, speaking from His heart and not our own. Being meek means representing God's strength, not relying on ourselves. "Most assuredly, I say to you, the Son can do nothing of Himself, but what He sees the Father do; for whatever He does, the Son also does in like manner."

Jesus said in John 5:20, "For the Father loves the Son, and shows Him all things that He Himself does; and He will show Him greater works than these, that you may marvel."

We develop meekness by becoming submissive and vulnerable to God. To know God's strength, we have to learn how to live in our weaknesses. We have to turn that weakness and inadequacy into vulnerability before God. When we stop crying out to God in hopelessness and begin approaching Him with thankfulness, we discover God's power.

Meekness is strength in the right places. The enemy subverts us in our excesses in the natural. When we have to use physical power to control people, we will crush them, use them, and abuse them. When we can only govern people by mental and emotional coercion then we are using the latent power of the soul, not the freedom-loving, gracious power of the spirit.

To live in the high places of the spirit demands a humility and a rest in the goodness of God. A meek person has been hugely overcome by goodness and loving-kindness to the degree that their own personality has been radically changed. That old domineering, overpowering personality has been thoroughly broken.

Meekness reveals and releases a different dimension of power, strength, and courage. Meekness shields us from the arrogance of our opposition while giving us an internal depth of authority that cannot be overcome. Meekness and rest, when combined, are very potent and powerful weapons. They are behaviors that dominate our lifestyle so that people may receive blessing. 2 Corinthians 13:4 tells us:

120

For indeed He was crucified because of weakness, yet He lives because of the power of God. For we also are weak in Him, yet we will live with Him because of the power of God directed toward you.

The context for this verse is that Paul must come to Corinth to bring a measure of discipline. It is the manner of his coming that he writes about. He will not spare anyone, but he is coming clothed in meekness.

We live with God in our weakness, and we live in Him because of the power that other people need to have directed at them through our lifestyle. What we are not in ourselves is used by God to bring blessing to others. His strength in our weakness makes us meek. Meekness is gratitude, humility, grace, and love combining fully in our heart and mind. It dispels our arrogance and opens us up to be a conduit for God's true nature.

Meekness is the high point of influence. It sees people's potential and speaks to it. It calls people up to a higher place of abiding, yet gives grace to people who choose a lower path of thinking. Sometimes people have to do it their own way, the hard way. We can stumble on the Rock and be broken, or it can fall on us and we are crushed [Matthew 21:44].

In meekness we get to stand with people now or wait for them to adjust later. Meekness empowers us to be consistent in our approach to people and circumstances.

We lead with influence and purity. Meekness allows us to sustain our innocence and not become cynical, sarcastic, or controlling. We seek the release of others, not their control.

In meekness, we relate to God more beautifully through all of life's provocations.

ASSIGNMENT

Examine your own heart and approach to people. How has the lack of meekness affected your own behavior? How has it affected relationships you have with other people? What must change in you; what must be broken that meekness may be birthed?

COMMISSION

Study Psalm 91.

Journal your thoughts on: the secret place, living in God's shadow, God as your refuge, living above the problem, living in the promise of God, and having God's love set on you.

PERSONAL NOTES

STRENGTHS AND WEAKNESSES ARE A PARADOX

Praise helps us to live in the right place. God is our inheritance—His nature is irrepressible and indomitable. He cannot be overcome. Our confession of faith must be in line with these truths about God's strength and provision, not our present condition. Our confession should revolve around who He is, not with who we are. We have to see ourselves as God sees us if we are going to be everything He wants us to be.

At first, Moses offered every excuse in the book as to why he couldn't possibly be the one to lead Israel out of bondage. In Exodus 7:1, God ended the debate: "See, I have made you as God to Pharaoh."

True to His word, Pharaoh was so bewildered by the power Moses wielded that he didn't know what to do or think. In the Egyptian king's limited understanding of the spiritual realm, he had no alternative but to conclude that Moses was some sort of god.

Gideon offered the same excuses at first. His self-image was a mess: "O my Lord, how can I save Israel? Indeed my clan is the weakest in Manasseh, and I am the least in my father's house," he said in Judges 6:15.

What did God see when He looked at Gideon? Read verse 12: "The LORD is with you, you mighty man of valor!"

Obviously, a significant gap existed between who Gideon thought he was, and what the Lord had laid out for him to do.

God bypassed every objection that Moses and Gideon gave Him. They were present to adjust to His perception of them. After all, He knew them better than they knew themselves. "Go in this might of yours, and you shall save Israel from the hand of the Midianites. Have I not sent you?" God said to Gideon in verse 14.

A spiritual warrior lives in this strength and weakness paradox. God always puts our weakness together with His strength. He does not ask us to be strong; in fact, our weakness is what attracts Him. He is strong enough for both Himself and us. He couples our inability with His provision.

This should be a rule in every believer's life: never talk about your own limitations without, in the same breath, magnifying the Lord that He is all-sufficient in His greatness. It is okay to be a grasshopper when we have a vision of how big God is.

Magnifying God is not an option; it is an antidote to poor self esteem. Our weakness is no longer a hindrance, for God sees it as an asset. This is not a logical concept, it is one rooted in intimacy and wisdom. The wisdom from above is spiritual, not intellectual. It impacts our heart and enlightens us so that we know what we can trust the Lord for in each situation. It is vital that our understanding is based upon God's nature and His way of perceiving.

Living out of the soul is a lower order of engagement because we are the prime focus. When we allow logic and emotion to lead us, fear grips us. But when we manifest our spirit, we have agreement and alignment with God. The Holy Spirit is not interested in what we cannot do; He is interested in what we are willing to do. If our heart is right before God, no present weakness can prevent us from overcoming the challenges before us.

God has given believers the gift of discernment of spirits. This ability enables us to determine what God has put into the spirit of His people, and helps us determine the location of the enemy. Whatever God has put in us must be developed. I know that when I walk into a room in my church, the level of faith rises. Why? Because I want to be a man who manifests his spirit, and I want to fight the enemy. When difficult situations are discussed in my church, I can raise the faith level by simply walking into a room.

"Fight the good fight of faith, lay hold on eternal life," [1 Timothy 6:12] was the verse given to me at my baptism as a young man. The officiate who baptized me did not believe the Holy Spirit still spoke today, and yet he essentially prophesied over me as a young man. God had put that fighting spirit inside me while I was still in my mother's womb. He knew the plans He had for me and even used a cessationist to speak them out.

A spiritual warrior's life, attitude, and perspective must be drawn from an internal source. If it's not, we end up looking for external stimulus at the time when we should be looking at who God is in our spirit. We cannot build a life by trying to correct weakness. Instead, we build our life by defining and refining the gifts, strengths, and revelation God has given us. "Therefore I remind you to stir up the gift of God which is in you through the laying on of my hands," Paul told his young protégé in 2 Timothy 1:6–7. "For God has not given us a spirit of fear, but of power and of love and of a sound mind." This is our starting point. Do this well, and by the end of the process, we will have trouble even remembering our area of weakness.

These strengths are the weapons that God will use in the warfare that swirls around us. They are the vehicle to victory that God wants to bestow upon us. When we focus on our weaknesses, we cannot make a difference in a critical moment. In fact, we may tip in the wrong direction! No one can inherit or possess a gift from God when they focus only on their weakness.

Every believer already possesses the things they need to both get free and stay free. It's already in us, put there by God Himself. We simply need to take inventory of our gifts and use that arsenal God has given us.

In Acts 3, Peter did not dwell on his weakness when confronted with a crippled man at the Gate Beautiful. Instead, he gave out of the strength God had put in him: "Silver and gold I do not have, but what I do have I give you: In the name of Jesus Christ of Nazareth, rise up and walk," [Verse

6]. The same principle was echoed by Paul twice in Philippians 4:

> *"I can do all things through Christ who strengthens me"* [Verse 13].

> *"And my God shall supply all your need according to His riches in glory by Christ Jesus"* [Verse 19].

When we pour out the blessing God has given us, another door opens for us in Heaven. We do not live out of a finite pool of anointing; God has more than enough to give us. He opens up realm after realm after realm of increase as we grow in Him. Prosperity then is about giving, not receiving. When we sow, God gives us both a massive harvest to reap and more seed with which to plant. We never eat our seed: this is a simple principle of life in Christ. We always sow and are lifted to another level of excellence. "The sharing of your faith may become effective by the acknowledgment of every good thing which is in you in Christ Jesus," says Philemon 6.

What has God put inside of you? What has He already given you? This is the starting place toward becoming a spiritual warrior. Mature Christians know both what God is doing *in* them, and what He is doing *through* them. They do not confuse the two.

What our souls see as crisis is actually an opportunity for expansion. It may have come in a strange way or a difficult time, but it is always an opportunity. Will we allow our soul to dominate in this time, or our spirit? Will we resolve to live from the right place? Are we determined to stand fast and rest in the Lord? These are the questions we will face over and over again in our lives.

ASSIGNMENT

🦁 Make a list of your weaknesses and a corresponding list of the strengths of God. Meditate on who God is for you. What must change in your mindset so that you may stand joyfully in the place of weakness and receive God's strength?

COMMISSION

🦁 Rejoice in your weakness! Let God come to you and be your strength. Do not try to grab strength from Him. Let Him be your strength. Begin to thank Him for who He is for you.

🦁 Step out and trust His strength to materialize as you walk. Trust Him for it. Describe the process and what you learned from it.

PERSONAL NOTES

LISTENING

It is undoubtedly true that we are the passion of God's great heart. When He looks at us, His heart is overwhelmed by love. This is as much true of us in our fallen state as it is through our place in Christ. Romans 5:8 states, "God demonstrates His own love towards us, in that while we were yet sinners, Christ died for us."

Out of the abundance of the heart, the mouth speaks. This is as much true of the Father as it is of people. Out of the abundance of His heart towards us, He speaks. His voice is connected to His heart for us. Fullness dominates His voice. His words pour into our heart in order to create in us the picture of how He sees us.

He loves us to hear His voice. To hear Him is to be healed—literally to be recreated in mind, heart, body, and soul. We should practice listening in tune with His speaking. His voice resonates with love. We must listen with love. His voice created the universe and shaped the world of mankind. His voice still brings everything into being on a continuous basis. He has not stopped creating. The universe is still expanding.

His ability to create new life in us is limitless. He delights to see us respond to Him. He speaks to us so that His own joy may enter our hearts and so that our experience of joy may reach its fullest potential [John 15:11]. He loves the rising joy in our hearts, the first few faltering steps we make towards delight. Every time He speaks, we smile. When we hear His voice, laughter should erupt in our spirit. Even when He gently rebukes us, our hearts cry with joy at His love for us in the midst of our flawed nature. When He has to chastise us, it is to prove conclusively that we belong to Him; we are His family [Hebrews 12].

There will never be a time when He will not speak to us. We must love the listening as much as He loves the speaking. He speaks to our heart to regenerate us, so that we may have total confidence and believe in the simple truth that we were made to hear His voice.

There is a divine capacity to hear His voice built into each of us. The Creator has designed a space within each of us whereby we may know His voice and respond [John 10:27]. The truth that will set us free declares to us that we are free to hear Him in our heart. We must therefore develop a larger expectation of hearing His voice.

His willingness to speak is greater than our ability to hear. His sheer pleasure in talking to us is bigger than our fear of hearing Him wrong. We must not doubt Him or we will doubt ourselves also. Never be in doubt; believing is always the better choice.

134

The Father will teach us to listen so that we can become confident. The beginning of confidence is that we believe in His delight over us—that He pursues us joyfully for our continual benefit. In His presence there is fullness of joy [Psalm 16:11], and that joy is our source of delight and happiness.

Then we must believe that we are designed with an inbuilt ability for our heart to respond and resonate to the sound of His voice. His goal is that we become confident in His desire to speak to us.

Delight is a wonderful part of our relationship with Him. He does everything from love and delight and teaches us how to delight in Him. His kingdom functions on joy and delight. He takes pleasure in His people [Psalm 149:4]. We are learning to be still, to be His Beloved, and to listen to His heartbeat. We must lose fear and regain delight as a way of relationship.

Are we not His people, His favorite, His pleasure? All that He asks is that we trust His heart toward us. The nearness of our God is our good. He put us into Christ, and we abide there as an act of celebration. The Father is delighted with Jesus; therefore, He is delighted with us having our inheritance in Him. We are the Beloved abiding in the Beloved. We should allow ourselves to feel His joy and delight.

Listening to His voice takes our heart to new levels of ownership in His presence. We are created to have conversations with Heaven. It is what we know as prayer—a love language that is made complete because it is mutual. Heaven always talks back! The Lord loves to initiate conversations and loves to respond to all that we say.

To speak, and not to listen in return, makes for an unfruitful relationship. We are called to bear fruit in all good things. I AM is speaking, and we are learning to listen from the heart, not our head. Listening is about utmost sensitivity and absolute intentionality. Connecting within our spirit to the inbuilt receiver that is Christ within. It is surely nonsense to confess that Christ is living within, and then to confess that we cannot hear His voice.

Prayer is Christ in us, praying to the Father, through the Holy Spirit. When we are simply still and at rest, prayer easily rises up within us—naturally spiritual and totally Christlike. When we are born again our receptor is switched on. If we want to hear God, we will. Love the listening. Love the anticipation of learning. Will we make mistakes? Sure! By far the biggest mistake is to believe that we cannot hear. We can start today. Begin rejoicing in the Truth. We can hear; God will speak; the Holy Spirit will teach us; we have Christ within; we are living in Christ and in God's delight. Have fun!

Don't try to think it; feel God's voice within. Listen in expectation. Practice, practice, practice. The more we give ourselves to something, the better we become at the practice of it and the more our experience matures. God will breathe on us. Enjoy the experience. Smile a lot. Take pleasure in learning.

The Holy Spirit will teach us to be still, to rest and be at peace. He will impart to us the ability to still the clamoring on the inside. The head noise will disappear as we learn to listen from the place of intuition in the hidden man of the heart. He speaks so that we will learn joy. We listen so that love may build up in our heart. He talks so that we may be edified, encouraged, and comforted by His voice. As a mother speaks to her infant, so God speaks to us so that we may know the soothing sound of His voice. As a child is made happy and comforted by the voice of a parent, so are we when God speaks.

As a mature person interacts with the voice of his Father, so we learn the conversations of Heaven, just as Isaiah did [Isaiah 6]. Hearing God is our right and our privilege.

ASSIGNMENT

What is the place of joy and delight that the Father wants to introduce to you in this season? What do you believe about joy and delight in the context of your walk with Him? How will you allow the Lord to develop your confidence?

COMMISSION

Practice joy. Practice celebration in Christ, rejoice! Practice feeling His voice in your heart. Be still and wait. If God does not speak initially, He will speak eventually. Love the learning. Feel the joy of His words. Experience the comfort and the encouragement. Allow yourself to be built up and nourished.

Write down what you hear.

PERSONAL NOTES

WE ARE ANCHORED BY PURPOSE

In battle, spiritual warriors are able to speak with utter confidence about God's ability. In every circumstance, they keep their gaze fixed on God. The story of the three Hebrew exiles in Daniel 3 is a perfect example of this principle. Shadrach, Meshach, and Abed-Nego refused to bow before a large statue of King Nebuchadnezzar. Until that moment, they had been loyal, trusted servants.

Enraged by even the rumor that the three would not bow, Nebuchadnezzar brought them before his royal court and demanded they bow. If they refused, they would be executed in a fiery furnace. The men didn't even flinch, as we read in verses 16–18 of Daniel:

> *O Nebuchadnezzar, we have no need to answer you in this matter.*
>
> *If that is the case, our God whom we serve is able to deliver us from the burning fiery furnace, and He will deliver us from your hand, O king.*

But if not, let it be known to you, O king, that we do not serve your gods, nor will we worship the gold image which you have set up.

Nebuchadnezzar could not believe his ears. He had demanded obedience, and he was humiliated in front of his own court. The three men knew their fate would be execution. They knew exactly what they were doing, but they had decided to live from a different place. They had given their entire being to the purposes of God, and they would not be swayed.

These spiritual warriors stood their ground, even as Nebuchadnezzar ordered the furnace's temperature to be multiplied seven times, as we see in verses 20–23:

And he commanded certain mighty men of valor who were in his army to bind Shadrach, Meshach, and Abed-Nego, and cast them into the burning fiery furnace.

Then these men were bound in their coats, their trousers, their turbans, and their other garments, and were cast into the midst of the burning fiery furnace.

Therefore, because the king's command was urgent, and the furnace exceedingly hot, the flame of the fire killed those men who took up Shadrach, Meshach, and Abed-Nego.

And these three men, Shadrach, Meshach, and Abed-Nego, fell down bound into the midst of the burning fiery furnace.

Simply being near the furnace killed the trio's guards. Opening the door should have incinerated the three Hebrews, just as it did the Babylonians. But the three did not die. In fact, they received an incredible revelation of God, when

He manifested His very presence in the furnace with them. He manifested His presence to them in such an awesome way that the circumstances were not allowed to touch them. His very fragrance prevented even their clothes from being tainted by smoke. Verses 24–25 tell us:

> *Then King Nebuchadnezzar was astonished; and he rose in haste and spoke, saying to his counselors, "Did we not cast three men bound into the midst of the fire?" They answered and said to the king, "True, O king."*

> *"Look!" he answered, "I see four men loose, walking in the midst of the fire; and they are not hurt, and the form of the fourth is like the Son of God."*

When we manifest our spirit, we can be put into places where we have no business being. Yet God is there. This courageous faith in Him leads us to get out of the boat and walk on water toward Him. It leads us into His presence, even in a fiery furnace, without a trace of fear. We have no ability to do these things — but God does.

Nebuchadnezzar was stunned by what he saw. He ordered the three to come out of the furnace, and they didn't even smell like smoke! The pagan king opened his mouth and praised God. Verses 28–30:

> *Nebuchadnezzar spoke, saying, "Blessed be the God of Shadrach, Meshach, and Abed-Nego, who sent His Angel and delivered His servants who trusted in Him, and they have frustrated the king's word, and yielded their bodies, that they should not serve nor worship any god except their own God!*

> *Therefore I make a decree that any people, nation, or language which speaks anything amiss against the God of Shadrach, Meshach, and Abed-Nego shall be cut in pieces, and their houses shall be made an ash heap; because there is no other God who can deliver like this."*
>
> *Then the king promoted Shadrach, Meshach, and Abed-Nego in the province of Babylon.*

These three spiritual warriors prospered for their principled stand against idolatry. When they had walked into that throne room, they had no idea what would happen. The consequences did not matter to them because they knew the calling of God.

Manifesting our spirit when we are frightened is the response of a true warrior. There are great days ahead of us, but we must be anchored in God to enter them. We have a journey to walk with Him.

God has not called us to be chocolate soldiers that melt in the heat of battle. Nor are we to be merely weekend warriors that dwell in meetings but not in life. He has called us to be men and women of substance. He wants us to manifest the things He has put inside of us, even in hard times. That to which He has called us will become real as we respond to Him.

The tests God sends our way are designed to establish what He has already put inside of us. The ability to pass every test is wired into us; we just need God's help to access those resources. Every problem comes with His provision. Every test comes with God's answer sheet attached.

Every believer has two choices when a test arises. They can choose to grapple with it using their mind and emotions; this will simply drive them further away from what God wants to be for them. Or the believer can take these tests in the spirit. When they rely on God for His provision, they move closer to Him. The test is present whether you acknowledge it or not. Passing or failing is mostly a matter of the will being engaged with God's purpose.

As we submit to God's purpose we may access what He has put inside of us. We can also experience what He has laid aside for us in this eventuality. A spiritual warrior passes every test with God's helping hand.

Crucial to the establishing of purpose is our rest and peace in the circumstances. There is no anchoring of purpose without rest and peace. Instead we become anxious in our thinking and may become subject to wild emotional mood swings. Philippians 4:4–7:

Peace guards our heart in the process of change. Rejoice in the Lord always; again I will say, rejoice!

Let your gentle spirit be known to all men. The Lord is near.

Be anxious for nothing, but in everything by prayer and supplication with thanksgiving let your requests be made known to God.

And the peace of God, which surpasses all comprehension, will guard your hearts and your minds in Christ Jesus.

There is always a process to follow as we learn to become more like Jesus. Rejoicing is at the heart of our life in God. Joy is the eternal disposition of God. Joy is who He is. Rejoicing is our response to who God is! In days of difficulty, rejoice twice as much. Rejoicing allows gentleness to emerge. We become softer in the presence of God, more gracious, loving, and kind. We view people as He does, and we rejoice in their actual resemblance to Jesus or in their potential to be different. Mercy reigns.

In this loving engagement, worry becomes an alien experience. We are no longer subject to anxiety because prayer is so enjoyable. Peace rules over us. We may not have full revelation yet about our circumstances, but peace comes from His presence—not our understanding of events. Peace guards our heart. Rest covers what we are not and allows us the serenity to become adjusted by God's nature.

We are made content by God's graciousness. We can look at our circumstances and bleat "I am not made for this". I am sure that was the concern of Moses and Gideon. Despite knowing the will of God and doing it, Gideon needed a ridiculous amount of reassurance, which God generously accommodated. The fleeces that He put out were not about guidance. The Spirit of God was on him, and he had already acted in response to God's will [Judges 6:34]. He simply needed to be more confident in himself when he met the men that God was sending to him. He knew they would be looking on him critically, expectantly, and with discrimination. He needed confirmation that he was the chosen one in these circumstances. The Lord's generous backing with the fleeces anchored Gideon in purpose.

When God calls us in weakness, He calls Himself to stand in our weakness, that we may experience Him in the low place of our self esteem. He steps into our vulnerability, and we experience an outpouring of who He is.

Peace is about the outcome, [Romans 8:28] which is guaranteed because of God's sovereignty. Rest is concerned with the process of how we get there. Peace empowers me to believe for the future. Rest enables me to partner with God in the present.

The enemy always overextends himself in persecution. He does not see the bigger picture that occupies God's perspective. Rest and peace enable us to both see the larger picture and know our place within it.

When we are anchored by purpose, we develop a predetermined response to situations. We do not wait for something to happen before we think about it. The three friends, in the court of Nebuchadnezzar, went into the throne room already decided on their response and in relative peace about it. They knew they would have no place of reflection, the king would require instant obedience. Their language contained no hint of being intimidated by the threats of the king. "God can deliver us from the furnace but even if He does not, we will not worship your gods or your image." They were totally anchored by purpose.

We are often not made for certain situations, but we are called to them nonetheless. As an introvert with a stutter I am not made for public speaking, but I am called to present truth in that way. My nervousness at standing before people is as high as it was at the beginning in 1972. It has not changed, and I still devoutly wish that someone else were called to this ministry. Nevertheless I am good at it. I have allowed God to be Himself to me. He has been my heart and mouth in public since those early times, and I have a confident expectation that He will speak through me and manifest His nature.

I am called to speak in public; mostly I rejoice over the call (90%), and I trust God for the rest. His purpose anchors my obedience. His goodness allows me to see all the benefits of our partnership in the changed lives of people with whom I connect in the kingdom.

ASSIGNMENT

🦁 What is God's purpose for you? What is the measure of peace and rest that you need to discover in order to anchor that purpose in your life? What is your pre-determined response that will anchor your purpose in faithfulness?

COMMISSION

🦁 Study Philippians 4:4–7. What is the process that you need to generate to move yourself more fully into God's over-arching purpose for your life.

PERSONAL NOTES

Personal Notes

DECLARING YOUR COMMITMENT

I have been both privileged and dismayed in my experience of churches around the world. The churches that I love and into which I could easily settle and live, have these things in common: they allow people to be themselves, and they have characters that are strong, unique, pleasant, and yet dangerous to the dark side.

They see themselves as relational communities where family and friendship are signs of the kingdom as much as wonders and miracles. People have fun and there is lots of laughter—the gentle joshing of people loved by God through people. Individuality and creativity are much prized, and the whole which we are cultivating contains a structure that is friendly, flexible, and inclusive. It is impossible to not see a place where you could connect and enjoy life. Everyone fits in and is empowered to discover their dream and practice their gifting on the people around.

It's a community of worshippers, believers who experience God. It is a community with many warriors, workers, and skillful practitioners of life and the arts. It is generous, fun loving, hard working, quietly restful, and Presence-focused. People are in Christ, learning to be Christlike. People are allowed to make mistakes and are given permission to grow and develop.

Contrast that with churches that are built on a functional paradigm. All the interactions are driven by task, vision, strategy, and purpose. They are geared to doing the most they can in the shortest possible time, with the least amount of resources. Buildings are developed to give people a nice physical environment. Programs exist where everything is done for you. It is a monoculture where we produce clones, not disciples. Individuality is not greatly appreciated, and true supernatural spirituality is not encouraged. Everything is planned, logical, and rational, but not spiritual, intuitive, or prophetic.

People are marshaled and taught to be consumers. There is an unwritten code of behavior, assumed rules, and hidden penalties.

Leaders in these places oversee the development of people spiritually but do not allow them to have encounters with God. They do not have the passion or the touch that empowers life to flourish in all its forms. In short, it is not led by the Spirit. It is full of good, not God, ideas. People are leaving there in thousands—not because they have lost faith, but because they need to find it.

The church is God's body, where every member is welcomed, accepted, loved, and valued as a contribution. There is room for us to live in Christ while we are learning to be

Christlike. This means we make space for the ugly and the beautiful in all of us to grow and change.

Everyone brings their abilities, gifts, intuitions, and desires to serve the kingdom and the community around our homes, hobbies, and places of work. The gaps and weaknesses in all of us are covered by individual and corporate love, grace, humility, goodness, and kindness.

It is a wonderful paradox that each of us is made complete by imperfect people. We learn that we are a general gift to many and a specific gift to some. All imperfect people are welcomed and loved on. We are as enthusiastic about the journey of others as we are with our own.

Good leaders facilitate; they don't control. We are bringing many sons (male and female) into glory and allowing them to become fathers (leaders/developers) of others.

In this wonderful, chaotic, life-enhancing, relational dynamic that is the Kingdom of Heaven acting on earthly people, we have the major relational issues of behavior and commitment.

Commitment is who we are regardless of circumstances. It is how we show up personally in Christ in the situations of life. It is not a choice. It is who we are, and who we want to be, combined together.

It is what we stand for when the chips are down. It is the values and principles we develop, so that we can learn to be as constant and as consistent as the Lord. Commitment is about our identity being revealed in every situation. It is the environment we create in all our relationships. Commitment is about how we want to be seen, known, and experienced by others. It drives our behavior, even the negative stuff that we are unlearning about ourselves. Commitment is our middle ground—the center of who we are, our inner man exposed to the light.

When we talk about commitment from a functional standpoint we relegate it to something we have to do. We apologize for not keeping our commitments. We talk about changing our commitment. We are committed to the idea of something but not always to the practice of something, as if that was possible.

Commitment is who you are in yourself. It is how you show up in a relationship or in a life situation. All circumstances are ultimately concerned with people and their commitments. Commitment is the very essence of who you are. You do not choose your commitment; you are becoming it. Manifesting your spirit is concerned with revealing who you essentially are now in Jesus. It is also about discovering your next upgrade in personality so that your commitment is empowered at a deeper level.

We are all engaged in the process of becoming who we are created to be. This is great! It is the core of our freedom—the right to make mistakes, learn, grow, and experience grace, goodness, and truth on the journey. We live in the love, peace, and gentle joy of God as we discover ourselves; and we enjoy the process of change in others.

To develop commitment we need to ask brilliant questions in the circumstances of life. One of my favorite ones that I ask the Father is, "What is it, that you want to be for me now that you couldn't be at any other time?"

What is this situation about? Every circumstance is set up for our profit [Romans 8:28]. The benefit may be experienced initially or eventually, but it will come, as we change and grow. When I ask that question I am inquiring of the Lord what He plans to give me of Himself. He loves to manifest His Spirit to us; and when He does, as we make it our own experience, we become different people.

Another question for me is, "Who do you want me to be with regard to my situation?" Which Fruit of the Spirit do I display? What part of the nature and character of God do I manifest? Some situations are primarily about my growth in Christlikeness. There are other purposes too, I am sure, but becoming Christlike is always near the top of any God-given agenda.

We are becoming our commitment. It is the expression of our commitment that strengthens or weakens. We are learning on a personal level how to be the best expression of who God made us to be in each situation. When we are who He wants us to be, we are in partnership with Him in His purpose.

Clearly there are differences between commitments and engagements. I like to make my commitments as purely about relationships as possible. We can be engaged with an undertaking and committed to the relationships specific to that appointment.

One of the branches of my ministry is consulting and resourcing groups of people through specific transitions. A transition is a seasonal device that enables us to engage with God in a defined way in order to achieve rapid growth in a specific area. It is a prime piece of spiritual real estate selected for particular development. In an organization it may be to develop a specific department or create a new one in a company. My task is well defined and my commitment is to the people within that undertaking.

I am not committed to the whole company relationally, but I am devoted to the specific people with whom I have a mandate to bring change. They get the best of me in the context of what we are doing, but I am also content for commitment to spill over into life. Commitment is who I am, not what I do. It is not a task; it is the essence of my personality.

I am commissioned to do certain events (conferences and training schools), some for people that I do not know personally. Often in the course of these engagements, life problems are occurring; people confide, and I am drawn into a more relational aspect of fellowship with them. People meet my commitment (who I am regardless of circumstances) and want to draw on it. Others want to make use of it in other ways.

In these situations I have to make it clear what my involvement will or will not be. Involvement is not commitment, but may lead to it. I want to be the best expression of Jesus that I can, within the limited scope of my involvement.

If you have a plumber in your house fixing your water pipes that burst in the winter, you probably would not ask him for financial advice, nor consult him about your pension plan or the stock market. You want a commitment to get your pipes fixed. You engage the plumber to complete a specific task. Most of western Christianity practices engagement not commitment. It is task-driven and only relational within the specific objective, goal, or strategy.

Heaven is not like that. Heaven is about loving friendships. The Godhead practices relationships with an agenda. The church undertakes a goal that involves relationships as a means to that end.

Perhaps the sin of evangelicalism is that we have put the Great Commission ahead of the First Commandment. Jesus came to restore Divine Order. Love the Lord your God with all your heart, soul, mind and strength. The Great Commission is the second commandment. Love your neighbor as yourself.

God seeks people to worship Him [John 4:23]. In worship we have brilliant encounters with God. The biggest battle at this time in the church is the battle for intimacy with God. True worshippers are people with a heart set on majesty. They are passionate about loving the nature and character of God. True worshippers know who God is for them. They know He is joyful, and they rejoice in His laughter and live happily under His smile.

Evangelicals mostly sing songs as a prelude to hearing the preaching of the Word. They are not taught rejoicing, thanksgiving, and praise. They know little of the deep places in worship such as high praise, lamentation, adoration, and how to proclaim. They seldom experience silent worshipful contemplation or the shouts of joy that emanate from around the throne. There are several distinct ways of moving in worship. True worshippers know them by experience and encounter.

The modern church is too functional to be intimate with the Lord. Worship is seen only as a means to an end—part of what it takes for a meeting to be deemed good.

It is a wonderful paradox that requires worshippers of God and laborers for the harvest. In a paradox, the question is this: what has precedence? The answer: Mary over Martha, worship more than evangelism. Jesus said "If I am lifted up (in worship, as well as sacrifice) I will draw all men to Myself" [John 12:32]. A paradox is two opposing ideas contained in the same truth. Mary and Martha are in all of us. Our life message is to be with Jesus and to respond to Him relationally. In the context of that intimacy we also serve the purpose of the Kingdom of Heaven.

That purpose is not just the redemption of souls through the Gospel of Reconciliation. It is to make disciples—people who follow Jesus properly. It is to raise up people to become Christlike in all areas of life. The fullness of the Great Commission is relational. It is connected to sonship, "to bring many sons into glory" [Hebrews 2:10].

This means specifically to teach people how to encounter God personally to such a high degree of relationship that their lives become glorious. We take on the nature and character of God in our hearts, minds, words, and actions. Commitment is the expression of that relationship. How we choose to show up in all our situations tells people who we really are. A thermometer measures the change of temperature. A barometer measures atmospheric pressure and is another indicator of change. Commitment measures our behavior to see if we are as unchanging as God. We learn constancy and faithfulness from the Lord Jesus. It is His behavior to be consistent.

If someone invites you to do something that is not true to Jesus, you resist. Our inner man knows our true identity. We are learning not to compromise our oneness in Christ. Great people are those whose commitment shines through the hardest of circumstances. It is how we manifest our spirit. We live our commitment, and it empowers us to breakthrough the expectations and the compromise.

Who do you become when situations do not work out the way you think they should? Who do you reveal when people and circumstances are against you? When you are betrayed, misunderstood, and threatened what do you manifest in that moment?

We cannot control our circumstances. They come at us how they will. We do not get any say in the how or what of life's trials. However, we do get a say in how we will respond.

If we get confused by our identity, the circumstances of life may overwhelm us, and we compromise our response to Jesus. Instead of it being a true and powerful expression of who we are, we show a different face. If we do that enough times, that face becomes a Christian mask. We display a veneer of Christ, but it covers an inferior material. A religious mask is a specious outward appearance of good quality that overlays an unsurrendered life. We are hypocrites. In less controlled situations we manifest our carnality, and we conceal our Christlikeness.

A truth not practiced is merely true because we are still bound. Only the truth sets us free. A truth believed, but not experienced, is a lie. 1 John 2:2–6:

> *. . . and He Himself is the propitiation for our sins; and not for ours only, but also for those of the whole world.*
>
> *By this we know that we have come to know Him, if we keep His commandments.*
>
> *The one who says, "I have come to know Him," and does not keep His commandments, is a liar, and the truth is not in him;*
>
> *but whoever keeps His word, in him the love of God has truly been perfected. By this we know that we are in Him: the one who says he abides in Him ought himself to walk in the same manner as He walked.*

When we fail to press into the nature of God we leave ourselves vulnerable to hypocrisy. Too much of that and we become religious and Pharisaical—self righteous and only concerned with rules. 1 John 1:5–10:

> *This is the message we have heard from Him and announce to you, that God is Light, and in Him there is no darkness at all.*
>
> *If we say that we have fellowship with Him and yet walk in the darkness, we lie and do not practice the truth; but if we walk in the Light as He Himself is in the Light, we have fellowship with one another, and the blood of Jesus His Son cleanses us from all sin.*
>
> *If we say that we have no sin, we are deceiving ourselves and the truth is not in us. If we confess our sins, He is faithful and righteous to forgive us our sins and to cleanse us from all unrighteousness.*

*If we say that we have not sinned, we make Him a liar and
His word is not in us.*

Uncommitted behavior can make a liar of God. When
we do not practice the truth, we make liars of ourselves and
it is possible for deception to ensnare us. In the context of
emerging life and change, our mistakes are honored through
fellowship and the blood of Jesus. The faithfulness (committed behavior) of God forgives and cleanses us.

When we allow life to frighten us; when we are anxious
and worried; when we get hurt, wounded, and resentful;
when we do not believe the best; when our desires and needs
are more important than others; when we control other
people "for their benefit;" when we view people as inferior—these are all forms of uncommitted behavior where
we do not reveal Christ but something else in His name.

Uncommitted behavior falls into four categories. Firstly,
we insist on being right and making others wrong. We do
not listen to others properly because we are convinced of
our own rightness. We hear what we want to hear. We do
not listen effectively because we are too intent on formu-
lating our reply. We ride roughshod over others' opinions
and ideas. We can use sarcasm and cynicism to quell what
we see as opposition.

Secondly, we are either dominating people or avoiding
domination. We control others for our purpose. We believe
God has given us people so that we can succeed. We use
people and often discard them when their use has been ful-
filled. People are either our possession or our opposition.
Sometimes God gives us relationships and partnerships that

are seasonal. A dominating person does not relate to people as partners, but followers.

When we are avoiding domination we do not display our truest identity. We moan and complain privately to others but do not confront in love the behavior of another. We fold our tents and sneak away rather than manifest who Jesus is for us. We go along with people and circumstances even though we hate what is happening. Our uncommitted behavior makes us a victim and weakens our own identity and destiny.

Thirdly, we blame others for events and are always trying to get ourselves off the hook. We delete, distort, and generalize as a way of life. We delete the memory of our own behavior and we distort the words and deeds of others in order to solicit sympathy and enlist support. When we are questioned we generalize on our own behavior but are specific about what we perceive has been done to us. When we excuse our own part in something and put the blame for the circumstances squarely on others, we are denying something fundamental in our relationship with God.

Of course, I am not speaking here of people who have been the objects of intense and focused, deliberate cruelty. It is, however, important that such people do not regard themselves as victims, because that thought maintains their degradation and will itself produce uncommitted behavior in later circumstances. Redemption redeems everything: past, present and future.

Fourthly, uncommitted behavior occurs when we justify our own bad behavior by the negative behavior of others. Reacting to people's behavior, instead of responding to

God's nature, means that we do not manifest what is true of Jesus in our spirit. We compound that error by drawing attention to what other people are not, in defense of our own uncommitted behavior.

Committed behavior is moving in the opposite spirit to the poor actions of other people. The Message version of Luke 6:27–38 says it all superbly!

To you who are ready for the truth, I say this: Love your enemies. Let them bring out the best in you, not the worst. When someone gives you a hard time, respond with the energies of prayer for that person. If someone slaps you in the face, stand there and take it. If someone grabs your shirt, giftwrap your best coat and make a present of it. If someone takes unfair advantage of you, use the occasion to practice the servant life. No more tit-for-tat stuff. Live generously.

Here is a simple rule of thumb for behavior: Ask yourself what you want people to do for you; then grab the initiative and do it for them! If you only love the lovable, do you expect a pat on the back? Run-of-the-mill sinners do that. If you only help those who help you, do you expect a medal? Garden-variety sinners do that. If you only give for what you hope to get out of it, do you think that's charity? The stingiest of pawnbrokers does that.

I tell you, love your enemies. Help and give without expecting a return. You'll never—I promise—regret it. Live out this God-created identity the way our Father lives toward us, generously and graciously, even when we're at our worst. Our Father is kind; you be kind.

Don't pick on people, jump on their failures, criticize their faults—unless, of course, you want the same treatment.

Don't condemn those who are down; that hardness can boomerang. Be easy on people; you'll find life a lot easier. Give away your life; you'll find life given back, but not merely given back—given back with bonus and blessing. Giving, not getting, is the way. Generosity begets generosity.

We move in uncommitted behavior for a reason. It feels good at the time. It's like scratching an itch. We get to prove that the other person was wrong all along, which is sweet, especially if they are aggravating us! We can get pushed to the end of our patience and come up with an opportunity that forces someone to do what we want.

Uncommitted behavior comes at a high cost, which is always too expensive. The enemy gets us both ways. Our poor behavior damages other people, and it prevents us from realizing our own identity. We are double losers.

Any behavior that does not take us forward into the nature of God must be discarded. Uncommitted behavior is the equivalent of going out and leaving the door open and the light on in our home together with a map showing burglars where all our valuables are located. Yes, it really is that dumb.

Uncommitted behavior has a cost to our relationship with the Lord, as well as people we want to be close to in life. There is a negative effect on our health, intimacy, personal joy, productivity, and our genuine self expression as a child of God. It also means we are not able to get closure on the past because our uncommitted behavior is more welcoming to the devil than it is to the Father.

There is no long term satisfaction in uncommitted behavior. All of life circumstances are allowed by God to empower us to manifest what God has put into our spirit. A fourteen year old Christian girl in India was raped by four men who hated her faith in God. As the fourth man was getting up off of her, she reached out her hand and touched his face, ravaged by disease, and prayed for healing. He was instantly healed. She is married with several children and has a powerful healing ministry in the southern states. In no way is she a victim, but she has become more than a conqueror. She manifested what was true in her spirit and the truth of that brought healing to an enemy.

As He is, so are we, in this world.

ASSIGNMENT

🦁 What are you committed to:

> For yourself?

> For your family/friends?

> For your local church/place of work?

COMMISSION

🦁 Is there an expression of uncommitted behavior that is a habit for you? What could you do instead that would be a better expression of your commitment? How would you move in the opposite spirit?

PERSONAL NOTES

PERSONAL NOTES

PERSONAL NOTES

THE WATER LEVEL IS RISING!... A PROPHECY

The water level is rising. I AM measuring you for a blessing. The enemy is measuring you for your destruction. I have measured you for your increase. The water level is rising around your life and circumstances.

As you partner with Me in this new day, I will soak your life with a fresh outpouring of My Spirit. I will soak your heart and mind with fresh revelation and impartation. The water level is rising around you.

The day of drought is at an end; the time of increase is at hand. There is a river flowing, and your life will be immersed in a fresh wave of life and anointing. You will no longer be damp, but drenched. I AM going to fill you with My passion, and you shall know the power of My intentionality.

Can you feel it, Beloved? Get into the river. Get into the river now! It does not matter if it is only a trickle, merely a stream. Get into it now, for the water level is rising. The level can only rise for you if you stand where I want you to stand; then it will deluge you.

If you stand on the outside, looking in, you will experience nothing. Come! Stand in the shallows, and the water will rise to a level where you will be carried away. This is not about being logical, but purposeful. I have not asked you to be reasonable, but faithful. Rationale is not required. Be spiritual and obey Me. Get into the water.

I will soak your life with a new passion. As you pay more attention to worship in this season, you will feel the weight of My desire for you, impacting your life. I AM going to indulge Myself in your life. This is a new day, a new time of upgrade and increase where you will move from measure to fullness.

There is new revelation available — fresh signs and upgrades in the supernatural. There will be life in all its abundance. I am taking the roof off your own life, your home, your business, and your spiritual community. Dare to believe that Heaven will come down.

It will not occur as in times past, for I am doing a new thing. In some places a dam will break, and the flow of anointing will carry all before it. In other places it will be a controlled breach by My Spirit so that the enemy may be specifically defeated. In still other places it will be a slow and steady rise and increase — the sign of a people moving from one level of power to another, from glory to glory.

I choose the outpouring; you choose the response. Seek Me; watch for Me; wait for Me. It has already begun. I AM creating space within you. The anointing is not external but internal. The impact is felt externally; the reception is an internal disposition.

I will create a clearing in your life so that you get closure on the past and position yourself for the future. Relax into Me and let Me create the space within so that I may overflow you.

My "Yes" is coming to you. It is here, and it is coming. Be affirmative in your response. Partner with Me or your feet will remain dry.

I will indulge My own goodness in your life. I will not deny Myself. Your life shall be full of My desire, and you will know My permission. I will dream in you. I will pray through you. I will ask over you. You shall knock, and I will open. I will not deny Myself. I will not withhold from you. Be confident; ask boldly. The water level is rising.

I have measured for you a blessing. I am saying "Yes!" to you. What is your question? I will say yes to your marriage, your children, your family. I will say yes to your finances, your anointing, and your promotion. Your prodigals will return in joy, and great will be their freedom.

It is time for an upgrade in your personality. The weak will become strong. The introvert will become bold. The extrovert will realize a new power in humility. The timid will overcome. The anxious will flow into peace and become powerful. The one who doubts will lead the way into miracles.

The confident ones shall access the High Places and see chariots of fire. They will do exploits and have a name like My sons of old: Abraham, Moses, Caleb, David, Daniel, and Mary.

You are My passion, and I will not deny Myself. You are My great love, and I shall indulge Myself. Ask Me for something bigger than you. Ask in line with your imagination. Ask beyond your thinking. I have abundance to give you.

I AM teaching you to dream, so that you may ask Me from the place of dreaming. Do not ask Me logically. I AM fulfilling dreams. The water level is rising. Come to a new attitude.

The river is flowing. Water is flowing from My throne. I AM making your place My place, and My face shall be your face. Stand in this place and open your heart to Me. I AM is standing in your midst. I have planted My feet in your place. I have stretched out My arms wide over you. I have taken the roof off. I want no covering between you and Me. You will receive glimpses of Heaven as it comes down to you. I will build My throne in your midst as you partake of new depths of worship.

Nothing shall be impossible for you in the River. I AM measuring you for blessing, for an anointing, and for fighting. You will overcome as you learn to fight using new forms of worship.

The water level is rising and will take you to the next place of your elevation. I AM going to romance you. I AM coming after you. Open yourself up in response. I AM saying "Yes!" to Myself, indulging My own desires. I will not deny Myself. I AM pursuing you to pour out My joy over you. You will hear My laughter and rejoice.

The sound of grieving, mourning, and weeping shall disappear. The sound of laughter, singing, and shouting for joy shall be heard in the Earth. It's time for praise and laughter. The water level is rising, and you must rise with it. You are

My portrait, My poem. I will sing over you, and your deliverance will create freedom around you.

Listen to My song and become it. Sing it back to Me around My throne. Let your heart resonate with it. The water level is rising; come up higher! I will sweep you off your feet, and there shall be no obstacle between us.

A certain sound has gone out into the Earth from Heaven. My people shall no longer be led by the sounds of their own making, but will resonate to the new sound that will come and is here already.

The water level is rising. Step into the deep place of God. Cast away your water wings and your flotation devices; get carried away in Me. Take the deep blessings of God. Take the fullness of your God. Bask in My intentionality and in My permission.

Say amen to Me, even as I say "Yes!" to you.

William Wilberforce has long been one of my favorite heroes. He fought his own government and high society in an epic battle to abolish slavery. He succeeded admirably. In 1833, the British Parliament passed the Slavery Abolition Act which gave freedom to all slaves in the British Empire. Three decades later it also became law in the 13th Amendment to the U.S. Constitution.

Today slavery is back and worse than ever. Former U.S. Secretary of State, Condoleeza Rice, stated that, "defeating human trafficking is a great moral calling of our time." It is a huge business, profitable to the tune of over $30 billion. Almost 30 million people are enslaved by it. Most are children; millions are sex slaves.

We need to raise up a new generation of abolitionists that can counter a worldwide epidemic. Human trafficking is a criminal enterprise that is international. It is sophisticated in its corruptive influence on law enforcement and government officials across the globe.

More slaves are in bondage today than were sold in 400 years of the slave trade that was abolished in the 1800's. Slaves are disposable people—like batteries: once they exhaust their usefulness, they are replaced.

What is required is a relentless pursuit of justice—a refusal to accept a world where one individual can be held as the property of another. For more than three decades I have financed projects around the world aimed at relieving suffering and creating a better quality of life. Fighting against human trafficking is different. It is not a project, it's more of a crusade. I want to affect things at a high level as well as on the ground.

If you want to give to Not For Sale (a campaign to abolish slavery) and partner with them directly, it's simple.

Go to their website www.NotForSaleCampaign.org, look at the range of what they are doing, and at the very least give a one-time gift, or give a monthly donation for six months or a year. Better still, involve your family, friends, business, or church in sponsoring a specific project.

Your contribution makes a world of difference to the people rescued by your involvement.

With heartfelt thanks,

Graham Cooke

Other Books by Graham Cooke

- Permission Granted (Co-authored)
- A Divine Confrontation (Out of print)
- Developing Your Prophetic Gifting (Out of print)

The Prophecy Series (Formerly Developing Your Prophetic Gifting)

- Volume 1 – Approaching the Heart of Prophecy
- Volume 2 – Prophecy and Responsibility
- Volume 3 – Prophetic Wisdom

The Being With God Series:

- The Nature of God
- Hiddenness and Manifestation
- Crafted Prayer
- Beholding and Becoming
- Toward a Powerful Inner Life
- The Language of Promise
- God's Keeping Power
- Living in Dependency and Wonder

The Way of the Warrior Series:

- Volume 1 – Qualities of a Spiritual Warrior
- Volume 2 – Manifesting Your Spirit
- Volume 3 – Coming into Alignment

The Wisdom Series:

- Secret Sayings, Hidden Meanings
- Radical Perceptions
- Keys to Brilliant Focus

ABOUT THE AUTHOR

Graham and Theresa Cooke reside in Santa Barbara, California. Working together with their closest friends, they have formed a kingdom community called Radiance.

Radiance is a community of creatives and entrepreneurs with a citywide focus on Arts and Business. While individual members of the community are involved in a wide range of kingdom activities (i.e. caring for the poor, teaching/training, pastoral ministry) the community, as a whole, is focused on impacting the social pillars of Arts and Business in Santa Barbara. They are committed to making a place for kingdom-minded dreamers to explore and realize the potential of their imagination—and to raising the "water level" of kingdom culture in the city.

He is married to Theresa who has a passion for worship and dance. She loves to be involved in intercession, warfare, and setting people free. She cares about injustice, abuse, and has compassion for people who are sick, suffering, or disenfranchised.

Graham and Theresa have a growing family spanning two generations and several countries. All their children are involved in business, the arts, or entertainment. There are numerous grandchildren who keep them busy laughing and enjoying life.

Graham is a popular conference speaker and is well known for his training programs on the prophetic, spiritual warfare, intimacy and devotional life, leadership, spirituality and the church in transition. He functions as a consultant and free-thinker to businesses, churches, and organizations, enabling them to develop strategically. He has a passion to establish the kingdom and build prototype churches that can fully reach a post-modern society.

A strong part of Graham's ministry is in producing finances and resources to the poor and disenfranchised in developing countries. He supports many projects specifically for widows, orphans, and people in the penal system. He hates abuse of women and works actively against human trafficking and the sex slave trade, including women caught up in prostitution and pornography.

Graham is an ambassador for communities of faith in the Body of Christ on behalf of Not For Sale. He talks about the work of Not For Sale and empowers individuals, families, businesses, ministries, and churches to get involved in sponsoring projects. Not For Sale has specific assignments that involve rescue, restoration, and providing education; skills based on training and small business development to enable people to become fully rehabilitated into a normal, productive life.

If you would like to invite Graham to minister an event, please complete our online Ministry Invitation Form at BrilliantPerspectives.com

If you want to give to Not For Sale and partner with them directly, go to their website: NotForSaleCampaign.org. Look at the range of what they are doing, and at the very least give a one-time gift or give a monthly donation for six months or a year. Better still, involve your family, friends, business, or church in sponsoring a specific project. Your contribution makes a world of difference.

Brilliant Book House

Brilliant Book House is a Vancouver, Washington-based publishing company founded and directed by Graham Cooke, and is dedicated to producing high-quality Christian resources and teaching materials. Brilliant Book House seeks to equip all of its readers to lead brilliant lives, confidently led by the Holy Spirit into the destiny God has for them.

We believe you have a unique call on your life that can only be found in God. He has something for you that is far beyond your wildest dreams. As you step out into that purpose, we want to stand with you, offering you encouragement, training, and hope for your journey. We want to equip you for what God wants to do in you and through you. That is our promise to you.

Brilliant is the culmination of a longtime dream of our founder, Graham Cooke. A thinker and a strategist, Graham is also a builder with a particular desire to establish resource churches that are prophetic, progressive and supernatural. Brilliant Book House is a key part of that call—producing books, journals, MP3s, e-books, DVDs, CDs, and other teaching materials.

For more on Graham, visit www.GrahamCooke.com.

> At Brilliant Book House, we believe you have a unique call on your life that can only be found in God. He has something for you that is far beyond your wildest dreams. As you step out into that purpose, we want to stand with you, offering you encouragement, training and hope for your journey. We want to equip you for what God wants to do in you, and through you. That is our promise to you.
>
> –Graham Cooke

Brilliant boasts an extensive collection of Graham's work. We distribute his CDs, MP3s, DVDs, books and Interactive Journals and offer a direct link between Graham and our customers through our newsletters, YouTube channel and podcasts.

Search for "Graham Cooke" on Facebook and be the first to receive updates on new projects, events and resources.

Brilliant Book House is a Washington-based publishing company founded and directed by Graham Cooke and is dedicated to producing high-quality Christian resources and teaching materials. Our vision is to equip all of our readers to lead brilliant lives, confidently led by the Holy Spirit into the destiny God has for them.

Brilliant has a passion for the Kingdom of Heaven, a powerful desire to see the Body of Christ comes into full dynamic stature in the Earth, and a hunger for everyone in Jesus to discover their rightful places in the purposes of God.

The world needs to see God in a *brilliant* way.

Visit us online today:

www.BrilliantBookHouse.com